TRANSLATIONS OF CHRISTIAN LITERATURE

SERIES VI

SELECT PASSAGES

SECOND-CENTURY CHRISTIANITY

SECOND-CENTURY CHRISTIANITY

CHRISTIANITY

A COLLECTION OF FRAGMENTS

BY

ROBERT M^c GRANT

LONDON
SOCIETY FOR PROMOTING
CHRISTIAN KNOWLEDGE
NORTHUMBERLAND AVENUE, W.C.2

First published 1946

FOREWORD

THIS little book is the result of a long and heartening letter which the Archbishop of Quebec sent me in December, 1941. In it he said, "I wish someone would publish a little corpus of these odds and ends which link the N.T. period with the developed catholicism of the end of the second century." Here is the little corpus, which I hope will prove interesting and useful.

The approach to each of the writers included has been as follows: first comes a brief introduction, then a quotation from Eusebius (if there is one) concerning the author, and then the fragments themselves. If the writer of any fragment has come to be regarded as heretical the relevant section in Pseudo-Tertullian (pp. 123-141) should be consulted. The articles in Smith and Wace's *Dictionary of Christian Biography* and the notes in Lawlor and Oulton's *Eusebius* will always prove helpful. Oulton's translation has always been compared with mine, and many of my errors have vanished in the process.

I am greatly indebted for help and encouragement to Professors H. J. Cadbury, F. C. Grant, A. D. Nock, John Knox, and S. E. Johnson, though most of all to Archbishop Carrington. But more than to anyone else this book owes its existence to my wife, who not only encouraged but also helped translate and type. To her it is dedicated.

R. M. G.

UNIVERSITY OF THE SOUTH,
SEWANEE, TENNESSEE.
April, 1945.

CONTENTS

(The numbers in parentheses refer to sections
of Pseudo-Tertullian)

INTRODUCTION

I.—VARIETY IN UNITY

WHAT we know of organized Christianity at the end of the first century is mainly the result of conjecture. We have a glorious theological picture of the Church in the Epistle to the Ephesians, but there are very few practical notices of its structure or activities in the New Testament. This is hardly surprising, for according to the theory of the canon all the works in the New Testament were written by apostles or their disciples, and most of them did not live to see the Church fully organized and at work. Even the author of the Pastoral Epistles, who writes in the interest of a regularized ministry, does not venture to give a great deal of detail, for he is writing in Paul's name.

As we enter the second century, however, the situation seems to change. From the Apostolic Fathers to the burst of literary activity at Alexandria, Antioch, Carthage, Lyons and Rome after 180, we possess (in addition to the great works of the Apologists, whose chief concern is popular philosophy and morals) many fragments of Christian literature, most of which are assembled in this volume. They include letters, sermons, exegetical works, books on controversial subjects. They are written by Jews and Greeks, by rich and poor, by administrators and theologians. To-day we hear much of the two hundred sects in America; but even they do not possess the variety of thought, on fundamental matters, which characterized the Christianity of the second century.

This variety was not only one of thought, however. It was a variety of geography. In addition to the churches of the first century (those mentioned in the New Testament, as well as Pella, Beroea in Coele Syria, Nazareth, Kokaba in

Basanitis, and some communities in Bithynia and Pontus), missionary activity resulted in the founding of the following churches: Rhossus near Antioch; Magnesia on the Maeander; Tralles in Caria; Philomelium in Pisidia; Nicomedia; Otrus, Hieropolis, Pepuza, Tymion, Ardabau, Apamea, Cumane, and Eumenea in Phrygia; Ancyra in Galatia; Sinope and Amastris; Debeltum and Anchialus in Thrace; Larissa in Thessaly; Lacedaemonia; Cnossus and Gorthyna in Crete; Sarau in Cephallene; Lyons; Vienne; Carthage; Scilli in Africa; Alexandria; Edessa; churches in Germany, Iberia, among Celts, in Egypt and Libya, in Sardinia, and below the Tigris; possibly also some in Persia. This list was compiled by Harnack, and nothing the student can do will be more useful than transferring it to some map of the Mediterranean world.

This geographical extension of the early church was bound together, however, by the travels of its leaders. Justin was born in Palestine but worked at Ephesus and Rome; his pupil Tatian went out from Mesopotamia to Rome, then to Antioch, and finally home again. Many other teachers came from their native provinces to the capital of the empire. Like St. Paul, they were great travellers. Indeed, a favourite piece of "Sunday afternoon literature" of the period concerns the various people Clement was said to have met on his trips —the so-called *Clementine Recognitions*.

Nevertheless it remains true that each of the great Christian provinces has its own characteristics. "The writers of Rome," says the Abbé Bardy (*Littérature grècque chrétienne*, p. 26), "are distinguished from the others by their practical spirit, by their sense of responsibility, by the firmness of their moral concern. The Egyptians, more idealistic, attempt vast syntheses; they try to explain the world, or at least to give general pictures of Christian teaching. The Asiatics hold above all to the transmission of the tradition they have received from the apostles, and struggle with an invincible firmness against heresies. Finally the Syrians and the Palestinians usually become chroniclers or historians, unless they draw up codes of liturgy or morals." Of course, this picture must not be pressed in too great detail, but in general it is valid for the second century.

II.—BACKGROUND: THE APOSTOLIC FATHERS

The Church's expansion was not merely geographical. It involved a literary activity which inevitably broadened and deepened its intellectual life; and this literary activity began early. From the "primitive" period we have remains which we call the writings of the "Apostolic Fathers." These include the letter of Clement of Rome, about 95; the letters of Ignatius of Antioch, about 110; the Teaching of the Twelve Apostles, probably from Syria, from the same period; the letter of "Barnabas," probably from Egypt, somewhat later; and the *Shepherd* of Hermas, at Rome, about the same time. The letter of Polycarp included with these works is possibly a composite writing, partly early (about 110) and partly a little later.

There was great diversity in the Church in this early period, even within single provinces. In Syria about the beginning of the century we find the Didache (Teaching of the Twelve Apostles) with its air of primitive freedom and emphasis on prophecy and apocalyptic; we find the rigid, fiery, episcopalian Ignatius with his passion for martyrdom; and we find the mystical Odes of Solomon, a hymn book of the early church which does not even mention the name of Jesus!

In Asia Minor we find a few bishops mentioned by name in Ignatius' letters; and one of them, his friend Polycarp, bishop of Smyrna, writes a sensible practical letter of moral instruction to the people of Philippi, warning the church there against those who deny that Jesus has come in the flesh. This denial was common in the Christianity of the East; along with it goes a dualism which separates God from his world. The Fourth Gospel, which states that "the Logos became flesh," may not have been ascribed to the apostle John at this time. The Johannine problem, however, is one that requires the making of books without end. We cannot discuss it here, though it is one of the important questions of second-century Christianity (see my article in *Harvard Theological Review*, April, 1942).

At Rome we find Clement writing in the Roman community's name to the church in Corinth and warning them against dissension, which results from jealousy. The Roman church is sending elders to Corinth to help them resolve their quarrel, and Clement concludes with a recapitulation of his teaching presented in the form of a prayer. Though the letter takes for granted the right of the Roman church to intervene in Corinthian affairs, this right is not vested in an individual. And while Clement regards the Roman church as apostolic, it is not clear that he bases its succession on Peter. To be sure he mentions Paul and Peter as the great modern examples of endurance; but he refers only to Paul either as a martyr or as having been at Rome. During the next forty years we find the prophet Hermas issuing a simple book of visions—probably first put out separately—then parables and commandments which were revealed to him by an angel of the Lord. His work begins in the form of a Greek romantic novel and is admirably suited to win the attention and respect of simple believers.

From these works we can put together some sort of picture of the Church as it entered the second century. It is not a uniform picture. Variety, even in a single area, is characteristic of the Church in the second century as in the first. There is no evidence at this time that from variety was developing uniformity (except perhaps for the efforts of Ignatius to maintain and extend the monarchical episcopate), except the uniformity or the solidarity of Christianity fighting the heathen world. This is especially true of what came to be called the Great Church, the majority, whose views were finally confirmed as orthodox. Well into the second century, however, there was within Christianity no sharp dividing line between what was orthodox and what was heretical.*

III.—SECOND-CENTURY CHRISTIANITY : THE FRAGMENTS

The fragments collected here come from many different schools within Christianity. I have omitted several groups in the belief that they were not Christian at all; Carprocates and his son Epiphanes were interested in Christianity only as an episode in the history of religions, and the Naassenes were so far from the main stream that they have little to offer readers interested in second-century Christianity. Notices concerning them, and concerning the other minority leaders, will be found in the *Against All Heresies* of Pseudo-Tertullian translated at the end of this book.

The first group of fragments comes from the highly educated and often wealthy "gnostics" of Alexandria, who were the first, and for a long time the only, Christians in Egypt. They were in search of something very different from the simple traditionalism of Asia Minor or the crude moralism of Rome. They were aware that, by the allegorical method, Stoic cosmology had easily been found in Homer, as

* See W. Bauer, *Rechtgläubigkeit und Ketzerei* (1934).

well as in the Bible of Greek-speaking Jews. They were acquainted with the popular dualism said to come from Persia. They had met reflections of it in the Old Testament. In other words, these Christians lived in the world of Philo. Yet after Philo we hear nothing of Jewish philosophy at Alexandria. Doubtless he had followers, but we do not know even their names. On the other hand, we do know that, after the revolt under Hadrian, Judaism practically vanished in Egypt, and Hellenistic Judaism died out everywhere. It is not improbable that many thoughtful Jews became Christians. At Alexandria they would naturally bring with them their old ways of thought and their exegetical method, which had already been foreshadowed in 1 Corinthians and Hebrews. It was doubtless they who had Philo's works copied. Such a movement from Hellenistic Judaism to Hellenistic Christianity would help account for the peculiar views of Alexandrian Christians.

The first Egyptian Christian of whose writings we possess any fragments is Basilides (I). He taught at Alexandria in the time of Hadrian, and claimed to be the disciple of Glaukias, an interpreter of Peter. There is no good reason to set aside his claim. Further notices of him, and of the other Alexandrian teachers, will be found in the notes to Pseudo-Tertullian, sections 4, 12, 13, 14.

Outside Egypt Christianity had less of a tendency to compromise with the world of thought or of government, with the result that most of the works of which we have fragments come either from controversies within or from attempts to win the world without. The earliest Christian apologist we know (outside the New Testament, much of which is implicitly apologetic in purpose) is Quadratus of Athens. "But the works of our Saviour were lasting: for they were real. Those who were healed, those who rose from the dead, were seen not only while being cured or while rising, but continued present; not only while the Saviour was with us, but when he had gone, they lived a long time, so that some of them survived even to our own times." Later apologists, such as Aristides, Justin, Tatian, Athenagoras, and Theophilus, were more sophisticated; but the appeal to miracle did not cease. Like Isidore (II), the son of Basilides, the apologists also devoted much space to showing that all ancient philosophy was stolen from the prophets. They tried to prove, too, the morality of Christian worship, which was constantly being attacked. Another apologist whose name should be mentioned is Melito of Sardis (XIII); but his ability is more evident in his homilies.

It may be said that most of the troubles of Asia in the second century were due to the Johannine writings. Montanism was based on the Apocalypse and Quartodecimanism on the Gospel. What Montanism was can best be discovered from reading the Montanist oracles and the two anti-Montanist works we possess (XXII, XXIV, XXV). Suffice it to say that it was by no means a return to primitive Christianity. It was the result of imperfect instruction of volatile converts, and the later form in which Tertullian could find it satisfying was very different from the original message which Montanus brought to Ardabau. Quartodecimanism was another matter. It was essentially a traditional usage of Polycarp and his circle. In the middle of the century he came to Rome to persuade Anicetus to take it up, but his attempt was amicably rebuffed. The question concerned the day for observing Easter. Was it always to be the 14th of the month Nisan? Or was it to be the Sunday afterward? The Asiatics, following Johannine tradition, held the first; the rest of the Church, as far as one can tell, the second. Eventually this second view prevailed. To us to-day such questions may not seem important. But to early Christians, especially Asiatics, anything involving the rites which the Lord instituted was

kindness of him who brought them. Though they may be accused on other grounds, they do not suffer like criminals condemned for what are admitted to be offences, nor are they cursed as adulterers or murderers, but as accused of being Christians. This will encourage them so that they will not seem to suffer. And if anyone who has not sinned at all happens to suffer (though this is unusual), such a man does not suffer through the machinations of power, but will suffer as a child would, who seems not to have sinned. As then a child who has neither sinned before nor has committed any actual sin now, but has sinfulness in him, receives good when subjected to suffering and reaps benefit from many difficulties—so also the perfect man, though he may not have sinned in act, suffers as a child while he is enduring afflictions. Though he has within him the sinful principle, he does not seize the opportunity to commit sin. He does not sin; but he is not to be reckoned as without sinfulness. For just as the man who desires to commit adultery is an adulterer, even if he does not succeed in committing adultery, and he who wants to do murder is a murderer, even if he is unable to kill; so also if I see the man without sin whom I mentioned suffering, even if he has done nothing wrong I should call him wicked because of his desire to sin. For I will say anything rather than call Providence evil." Then he speaks of the Lord as of a man: "If then, passing on from all these observations, you were to proceed to confound me by saying, concerning someone or other, 'This man, then, has sinned, for this man has suffered'; if you permit, I will say, 'He has not sinned, but was like a child suffering.' If you were to insist more urgently, I would say that 'Whatever man you name is man, but God is righteous; for no one is pure, it is said, from pollution' [Job xiv. 4]." (Clement Alex., *Stromata*, iv. 12. 81.)

3. 'I,' says Paul, 'am dead' [Rom. vii. 10]: for now sin

begins to be reckoned to me. But Basilides, not noticing that this must be understood of the law of nature, turns the apostle's word into stupid and irreligious fables, and tries to expound this word of the apostle as concerning metempsychosis, that is, the doctrine that souls transmigrate from body to body. "For the apostle said, 'I formerly lived apart from law' [Rom. vii. 9], that is, before I came into this body I lived in that kind of body which was not under law, that of a beast or a bird." (*Ibid.* 82.)

4. "We suppose one part of what is called the will of God to be to love all things, because all things bear a relation to the whole, and another, not to desire anything, and a third, not to hate anything." (*Ibid.* 83.)

5. "We are men, and the others are all swine and dogs; therefore it says, 'Cast not pearls before swine nor give that which is holy to the dogs' [Matt. vii. 6]." (Epiphanius, *Haer*. xxiv. 5.)

FOLLOWERS OF BASILIDES

6. "When the apostles asked whether it was better not to marry, they say the Lord answered, 'Not all can keep this word, for there are some who are eunuchs from birth, others from necessity' [Matt. xix. 11 *f.*]. They expound the saying thus: Some have a natural aversion to women from birth, and they make right use of this natural temperament by not marrying. Eunuchs from necessity, the fighters in the arena, are continent for the sake of glory. [Then also those who have been castrated by some accident are eunuchs from necessity.] Then those who are so from necessity are not eunuchs according to reason; but those who become eunuchs for the eternal kingdom do so to avoid the consequences of marriage; they fear the burden of acquiring all that is necessary. 'It is better to marry than to burn' [1 Cor. vii. 9] means: Do not throw your soul into fire by resisting night and day and

fearing lest you fall from continence. For while the soul is occupied in resisting it cuts itself off from hope." (*Strom*. iii. 1. 1).

Agrippa Castor

7. Among the works which have come down to us, there is a most powerful refutation of Basilides by a writer of the greatest renown at that time, Agrippa Castor, which unmasks the man's cunning imposture. In exposing his hidden mysteries, he says that Basilides composed twenty-four books on the Gospel, and on the other hand that he named Barcabbas and Barcoph as his prophets, providing himself likewise with certain others who never existed, whom he called by barbarous names in order to strike amazement into those who marvel at such things; that he taught that to taste meat offered to idols, and to renounce without reservation the faith in times of persecution, were matters of indifference; and that he imposed upon his followers a five years' silence after the manner of Pythagoras. (*H.E.* iv. 7. 11. Barcoph= Parchor; see Isidore, 3.)

II.—ISIDORE

Basilides' son Isidore continued his father's teaching at Alexandria and apparently drew farther away from the main stream of Christianity. His fragments seem to favour a combination of rationalistic ethics and theological learning.

Ethics

1. "Resist a passionate woman, lest you be torn away from the grace of God; and having driven out the fire, pray with a good conscience. But when your thanksgiving gives way to petition, and furthermore your desire in the future is not to succeed but not to sin either, then marry. But in the

case of a youth or a pauper or a sensual man, who with reason does not wish to marry, let him not spurn his brother; let him say, 'I have entered into the holy things; I have no passions.' If he has some uncertainty let him say, 'Brother, lay your hand on me lest I sin'; and he will receive help both in mind and in body. Let him desire only to accomplish good, and he will attain. But sometimes we say with our mouth, 'We do not desire to sin,' but our mind is intent on sin. Such a one through fear does not do what he wants, lest punishment be reckoned to him. But human nature has things that are necessary and natural for it. To need clothing is necessary and natural; the need of sexual pleasure is natural but not necessary." (*Strom.* iii. 1. 2 *f.*)

On the Adhering Soul

2. "For if you persuade anyone that the soul is not indivisible, but that the passions of the wicked come from the force of the appendages, the worthless among men have no small pretext for saying, 'I was forced, I was carried away, I did it unwillingly, I acted against my will'; yet he himself was the leader of his desire for evil things, and did not fight against the force of the appendages. But it is necessary for us to acquire superiority by our reason and to show ourselves masters of the inferior creation within us." (*Ibid.* ii. 20. 113 *f.*)

Expositions of the Prophet Parchor [*Barcoph*]

3. (*Book I*) "The Attics say that certain things were intimated to Socrates by a demon attending him. And Aristotle says that all men are provided with demons who attend them while they are in the body; he takes this instruction from the prophets and transfers it to his own books without confessing where he got this statement." (*Book II*) "And let no one think that what we call peculiar to the elect was said earlier

by any of the philosophers. For it is not their discovery; they appropriated it from the prophets and attributed it to him whom alone they call wise. . . . For to me it appears that those who profess to philosophize do so in order to learn what the winged oak is, and what the cloak embroidered on it —all of which Pherecydes used as theological allegories, having taken the prophecy from Ham." (*Ibid*. 6. vi. 53.)

"Zeus makes a great and beautiful cloak and on it embroiders the earth and ocean and the palace of Ocean" —Pherecydes, in *Strom*. vi. 2. 9; see Grenfell and Hunt, *Greek Papyri*, ser. ii, no. 11. Compare Wisdom xviii. 24: "For upon the garment down to the feet was the whole world."

"One of the family of Noah was named Ham. . . . The people who lived then called him Zoroaster, admiring him as the first founder of the art of magic; in his name there are many books in addition to this one."—*Clementine Recognitions* iv. 27.

III.—VALENTINUS

Valentinus, who taught first at Alexandria and then at Rome, was the greatest of the rationalistic teachers of the second century. He claimed a succession from Paul's disciple Theodas. His letters are theological in nature. The first explains the reason for human imperfection; the second shows how the heart becomes pure when the Father visits it and drives out the demons which live in it; the third, to a certain Agathopous, describes the docetic Jesus. The fourth fragment, from a homily, explains the world in Platonic terms. In the fifth fragment, from a tractate, the case for "natural religion" is briefly stated. The sixth and seventh fragments, from Hippolytus, show the religious origin of Valentinus' thought, while the eighth, from a psalm, demonstrates its theosophical development. Pseudo-Tertullian discusses him in section 12.

Letters

1. "And as fear of this creature fell on the angels, because he uttered things greater than were suitable to his creation, on account of the one who had invisibly put in him a seed of the substance from above, and who spoke with free utterance, so also among the tribes of men in the world, the works of men become terrors to those who have made them—for example, statues and images, and everything which hands fashion to bear the name of God: for Adam, having been formed into the name of man, inspired the fear attaching to the pre-existent Man, who had his being in him; and they [the angels] were terror-stricken, and rapidly marred the work." (*Strom.* ii. 8. 36.)

2. "There is one Good, whose presence is manifested by the Son. By him alone can the heart become pure, by the expulsion of every evil spirit from the heart; for the many spirits dwelling in it do not allow it to be pure, but each of them performs his own deeds, insulting it often with unseemly lusts. And the heart seems to me to be treated somewhat like an inn, for that has holes and ruts in it, and is often filled with dung by men who live filthily in it and take no care of the place since it belongs to others. So it happens with the heart as long as there is no thought taken for it; it remains unclean and the abode of many demons. But when the Father, who alone is good, visits it, it is sanctified and gleams with light. And he who possesses such a heart is so blessed that 'he shall see God' [Matt. v. 8]." (*Ibid.* ii. 20. 114.)

Letter to Agathopous

3. "Having endured everything he was continent; thus Jesus exercised his divinity. He ate and drank in a peculiar manner, not evacuating his food. So much power of

continence was in him that in him food was not corrupted, since he himself had no corruptibility." (*Ibid*. iii. 7. 59.)

A Homily

4. "From the beginning you have been immortal, and children of eternal life; and you wanted to share death among yourselves in order to consume it and spend it, so that death might die in you and by you. For when you dissolve the world and are not yourselves dissolved, you are lords of creation and of all corruptible things. . . . As much as the image is inferior to the living face, so much is the world inferior to the living Aeon. What is the cause of the existence of this image? It is the greatness of the face, which provides the type to the painter so that it may be honoured by his [the model's] name. For a form by itself is not authentic; the name supplies what is lacking in the likeness. So, too, the invisibility of God works to uphold the faithfulness of that which has been formed." (*Ibid*. iv. 12. 89.)

On the Conversation of Friends

5. "Many of the truths written in ordinary books are found written in the Church of God; for these are common words from the heart—the law written in the heart. This is the people of the Beloved One, which is loved by him and loves him." (*Ibid*. vi. 6. 52.)

6. "All the prophets and the Law spoke from [the inspiration of] the Demiurge, a foolish god; they themselves were fools who knew nothing. For this reason the Saviour declares, 'All who came before me were thieves and robbers' [John x. 8], and the apostle says, 'The mystery which was not known to former generations' [see Col. i. 26]. For none of the prophets declared anything concerning the matters of which we speak." (Hippolytus, *Ref*. vi. 35. 1.)

7. Valentinus says he saw a new-born child, and questioning it he asked who it might be. It answered and said it was the Logos. Thence forming some tragic myth, he wants his attempted heresy to consist of this. (*Ibid*. vi. 42. 2.)

A Psalm

8.   "I behold all things hanging from spirit of aether,
      I perceive all things upheld by spirit,
      Flesh hanging from soul,
      Soul standing forth from air,
      And air hanging from aether;
      But fruits borne away from Bythos [Depth],
      But the embryo from the womb."

                              (*Ibid*. vi. 37. 7 *f*.)

IV.—A VALENTINIAN TRACTATE

The theosophical nature of Valentinianism is well portrayed in this fragment preserved by Epiphanius (*Haer*. xxxi. 5 *f*.). A strange combination of mythology and number-mysticism, it is perhaps a homily addressed to the "never-ceasing ones". Only that part of the tractate translated by H. Liesegang in *Die Gnosis* is translated here; the remainder is not different in character.

"Never-ceasing Nous to the never-ceasing ones, greeting.

"I am going to discuss with you nameless and unspeakable and superheavenly mysteries, which are subject neither to principalities nor to powers nor to subjects nor to anything which can be understood by the intelligence, but can be revealed only by the Thought of the Changeless. For when in the beginning the Father himself held all things in himself, which rested in him without consciousness—in him whom they call the never ageing, eternally young, male-female Aeon, who everywhere surrounds all things and yet is not surrounded by them—then Thought contained in him (that power whom some call Thought, others Grace—and to be sure quite rightly, for she has graciously relinquished treasures of Greatness to those who stem from Greatness—and others correctly call her Silence, because Greatness completed all things through thought without words)—then, as I was saying, immortal thought desired to break the eternal bonds, and aroused the tendency of Greatness toward marriage, from longing to lie with her. And when she had had intercourse with Greatness, she brought forth the Father of Truth to light, one whom the perfected rightly named Man because he was the type of the unbegotten-before-all-being yet to come. After this, Silence incited the physical union of Light with Man (their coming together existed by her will alone) and brought forth Truth. Truth is rightly so called by the perfected because in truth she was like her mother Silence, who desired lights to be divided equally into male and female, so that through the lights themselves the unity actually in them might be manifest in those of them who were [merely] lights visible to the senses. After this there was aroused in Truth the lustful tendency of her mother, and she attracted the attention of her father to herself, and they lived together, and in immortal intercourse and in never-ageing fusion they brought forth the pneumatic male-female tetrad, the type of the pre-existent tetrad which is composed of Depth, Silence, Father, and Truth. This [former] tetrad descended from Father and Truth is composed of Man, Church, Logos, and Life. Then, by the will of all-surrounding Depth, Man and Church were united, mindful of the Father's words, and brought forth the Dodecad of the productive male-female beings. The male beings are Helper, Paternal, Maternal, Eternal, Wilful (who is Light) and Ecclesiastical; the female are Faith, Hope, Love, Intelligence, Blessedness, Wisdom. After these come Logos and Life. They remodelled the gift of unity and had fellow-ship with each other (their fellowship is volition), and brought forth a decad of productive male-female beings. The male beings are Deep, Ageless, Self-Existent, Only-Begotten, Immovable (these took their names for the glory of the All-Surrounding). The female are Intercourse, Union, Blending, Unity, Pleasure (and these took their names for the glory of Silence). When then according to the will of the Father of Truth the Thirty was perfected, who is the Number that mortal men on earth count, without knowing anything about her, and with whom they turn round and begin to count again (when they have reached her and cannot count beyond [*i.e.*, days of the month])—she is composed of Depth, Silence, Father, Truth, Man, Church, Logos, Life, Helper, Paternal, Maternal, Eternal, Wilful, Ecclesiastical, Faith, Hope, Love, Intelligence, Blessedness, Wisdom, Deep, Ageless, Self-Existent, Only-Begotten, Immovable, Inter-course, Union, Blending, Unity, Pleasure—then the All-Surrounding resolved, in unsurpassable understanding, to call forth another Ogdoad opposite the authentic pre-existent one, though remaining within the number of Thirty, and he placed the male numbers opposite to the male beings—the One, the Three, the Five, the Seven; and the female opposite the female—the Two, the Four, the Six, the Eight. This then is the Ogdoad which was called forth from the pre-existent Ogdoad, that is, that composed of Depth, Father, Man, Logos, and Silence, Truth, Church, Life; and it was united with the lights. So arose the separated Thirty. The pre-existent Ogdoad, however, remained composed and at rest." (Epiphanius, *Haer.* xxxi. 5 *f.*)

V.—PTOLEMAEUS

Ptolemaeus (about 160) is the Valentinian whose fragments impress the modern reader most favourably. His letter to Flora, probably taken by Epiphanius from the same source in which he found the Tractate (IV), reflects careful thought and a clear understanding of the problems presented by the Old Testament to the new Christianity. Had his threefold division been accepted by the early Church the problem of modern criticism might have been much less pressing, especially during the late nineteenth century.

The commentary on the prologue to the Fourth Gospel shows some of the sense of the letter to Flora, but tries to introduce Valentinian tetrads and ogdoads into the gospel.

Ptolemaeus is discussed in Pseudo-Tertullian 13.

Letter to Flora

1. "The law given through Moses, my dear sister Flora, which many do not understand, knowing neither its origin nor its commandments, I think you will easily understand if you learn the varying opinions about it. There are those who say it was ordained by God the Father; others, on the contrary, assert that it was laid down by the hostile and corrupting devil, to whom they attribute the creation of the world, calling him its father and creator. But those who recite this to one another are quite wrong, and in both ways they go astray from the evident truth. For it appears that this was not established by God the Father—it follows from the nature of the Law, which is imperfect and lacks its own completion, and has commandments alien to the nature of such a God; nor again is the Law to be attributed to the unrighteousness of the adversary, who chose to do wrong. Both of these opinions follow from not paying attention to what was said by the Saviour. For 'a house or city divided against itself cannot stand' [Matt. xii. 25], our Saviour

declared. Furthermore the apostle says the creation of the world was his ('All things were made through him, and apart from him was made nothing' [John i. 3]), refuting the flimsy wisdom of these liars; not the creation of a death-dealing god, but of a just one who hates evil. That is the opinion of heedless men who do not understand the cause of the providence of the Demiurge, who seem to be blind not only in the eye of the soul but also in that of the body. How they have strayed from the truth is clear to you from what has been said. Two groups have introduced their own views, some through ignorance of the Father of All, whom only he who alone knew him revealed at his coming. Now it remains for us to consider the opinions of both of these, and to explain and clarify the Law to you, what its nature is, and the one by whom it was given, the Lawgiver, proving our demonstrations from the words of our Saviour, through which alone without error we can travel toward the comprehension of things."

2. "First one must know that that whole Law which is contained in the Pentateuch was not decreed by some one person, I mean by God alone; but there are also some ordinances in it given by men; and that it is tripartite the words of the Saviour teach us. For one part is ascribed to God himself and his legislation; another is ascribed to Moses, not as God gave the law through him but as Moses legislated from his own understanding; and the third is ascribed to the elders of the people, who first ventured to introduce certain ordinances of their own. How this came about you may learn from the words of the Saviour. When the Saviour was talking somewhere to those who came to question him about divorce, which was allowed by the Law, he said to them, 'Moses because of the hardness of your hearts permitted a man to put away his wife; from the beginning it was not so' [Matt. xix. 8]. For God joined them together, and 'what God hath

joined, let no man put asunder' [Matt. xix. 6]. Here he shows that the law of God is one thing—it forbids a woman to be divorced by her husband—and the law of Moses is another—it permits the breaking of the bond because of hardness of heart. Then in this matter Moses ordained a law contrary to God, for divorce is contrary to no divorce. But if we examine carefully the opinion of Moses, according to which he made this law, we find that he did not do this of his own choice but of necessity because of the weakness of those for whom he legislated. For since they could not achieve the will of God, who forbids them to divorce their wives, with whom some of them lived in incompatibility, they stood in danger of falling into greater wrongdoing and from this into annihilation; and, desiring to free them from this dreadful situation, through which they might have perished, Moses substituted a second law for the critical times, a less for a greater, and of his own accord decreed the law of divorce for them, so that if they could not keep the other and yet could keep this they might not fall into wrongdoing and evil, which would have led them to annihilation. This was his opinion, in which he is found to be legislating against God. That this law of Moses was different from the Law of God is beyond doubt, if we have proved it only at this point. Now that there are some traditions of the elders bound up with the law, the Saviour makes clear. For 'God said, Honour thy father and thy mother, that it may be well with thee. But ye call,' addressing the elders, 'a gift to God whatever might have profited thee from me, and ye make void the Law of God by the tradition of your elders.' This Isaiah also cried out, saying, 'This people honoureth me with their lips, but their heart is far from me. But in vain do they worship me, teaching as their doctrines the precepts of men' [Matt. xv. 4-9). Clearly then from these (examples) the whole Law is proved to be divided into three parts; we find in it the legislation of Moses himself, and of the elders, and of God. And this division of ours, of the whole Law, shows its own truth to us."

3. "Again that part of the Law which is from God himself is divided into three parts, into pure legislation, free from evil, which is rightly called Law and which the Saviour 'came not to destroy but to fulfil' [Matt. v. 17] (for that which he fulfilled was not alien from him, or else it could not have been perfected); and into that part bound up with lower things and wrongdoing, a law which the Saviour abrogated as alien to his nature; and it is divided also into that part which is typical and symbolical, legislated as images of higher spiritual things, which the Saviour transformed from the sensible and phenomenal into the spiritual and invisible. And that pure law of God, free from evil, is none other than the Decalogue, those ten sentences divided into two tablets, for the prohibition of things not to be done and the injunction of things to be done—which though they are pure legislation do not reach perfection, for they lacked fulfilment by the Saviour. The second kind which is bound up with wrongdoing and concerned with vengeance and retribution for previous wrongs contains and orders payment of 'an eye for an eye and a tooth for a tooth and a death for a death' [Deut. xix. 21; cf. Matt. v. 38]. For the second wrongdoer is not less unrighteous; he differs only in sequence while he does the same deed. But this commandment was and is just, insofar as it is necessary for the weakness of those for whom the legislation was made, though it deviates from the pure Law, and is alien to the nature and goodness of the Father of all; and it may be even more suitable because of the force of circumstances. For when he who forbids a single murder, saying 'Thou shalt not kill' [Deut. v. 17], orders the murderer to be murdered, lays down a second law, and commands a double murder—he who had forbidden one—he forgot himself, overwhelmed by circumstance. Therefore the Son sent by him took away

that part of the law, though he admitted it was from God, both in those parts ascribed to the ancient sect [Judaism] and in those in which God had spoken, saying, 'He who curses father or mother shall surely die' [Exod. xxi. 17]. Then there is the third part of it, which is typical, in the likeness of spiritual and more excellent things, namely the laws of sacrifice and circumcision and Sabbath and fasting and Passover and unleavened bread, and legislation on such matters. All these things, being images and symbols, were transformed when the truth was made manifest. The material performance according to appearance was taken away, but revealed according to the spiritual—the names remained the same but the deeds were different. For the Saviour commanded us to offer sacrifices, but not of irrational animals or incense but of spiritual praises and gloryings and thanksgiving, and through fellowship and beneficence toward neighbours. And he wants us to be circumcised, not by the material circumcision of the foreskin, but by the spiritual circumcision of the heart; and to keep the Sabbath, for he wants us to keep away from evil deeds; and to fast, but he wants us not to keep a bodily fast but a spiritual, one in which there is the avoidance of all bad things. But indeed our people should also keep the outward fast, since it may bring something to the soul when it is done with reason and not in imitation of others nor for custom, nor because of a day, as if it were appointed for this purpose; but for a reminder of the true fast, so that those who are not able to keep that may have a reminder of it through the outward fast. And similarly Paul the apostle shows that the Passover and the unleavened bread are images, saying, 'Christ our Passover has been sacrificed,' and he continued, 'So that ye may be unleavened, not having leaven' (by leaven he means evil) 'but may be new dough' [1 Cor. v. 7 f.]."

4. "Thus the Law of God itself is divided into three parts:

into that fulfilled by the Saviour, for the 'Thou shalt not kill, thou shalt not commit adultery, thou shalt not swear falsely' was fulfilled in the commandments not to be angry nor to lust nor to swear an oath. Another part was that taken away completely; for the 'An eye for an eye and a tooth for a tooth', bound up with wrongdoing and itself containing the word of unrighteousness, was taken away by the Saviour through its opposite (opposites are destructive of each other). 'For I say unto you, Resist not evil at all, but if anyone strikes you, turn the other cheek also to him' [Matt. v. 39]. Now the symbolical part is allegorical of what is transformed and changed from bodily into spiritual; it was given as law as an image of the things above. For the images and symbols were good, insofar as they were representative of other things, as long as the truth had not yet appeared; but when the truth appears, one must do the deeds of the truth, not those of the image. These things his disciples and the apostle showed, exhibiting for us the image-part of the law, as we have already said, by the Passover and the unleavened bread; the part of the law bound up with wrongdoing, in the saying, 'The abolition of the law of commandments contained in ordinances' [Eph. ii. 15]; and finally the part not connected with inferior things, in the saying, 'The law is holy and the commandment holy and righteous and good' [Rom. vii. 12].''

5. ''In short, then, I think I have shown you sufficiently both the legislation introduced by men and the threefold division of the Law of God. There remains for us the question, Who is this God who gave the Law? But I think this also has been shown you from the preceding remarks, if you have paid close attention. For if the Law was given neither by the perfect God himself, as we have taught, nor by the devil, a thing which it is not right to say, someone other than these two must have given the Law. And he is

the Demiurge and creator of this whole world and what is in it, and he is different from the nature of those two; standing as a mediator between them, he should rightly bear the name 'the middle.' And if that perfect God is good by his nature, as he is ('For one only is the good God' [Matt. xix. 17], our Saviour said of his Father whom he revealed), and if the evil and wickedness of the adversary's nature is characterized by unrighteousness, then he who stands between them as a mediator, and is neither good nor bad nor unrighteous, may correctly be called righteous, since he is the bearer of righteousness. And this god will be lower than the perfect God and less than his righteousness, for indeed he is also begotten and not unbegotten—for one is the unbegotten 'Father, from whom everything' [Eph. iii. 14, cf. iv. 6] is, since everything was fashioned by him, but he will become greater and more powerful than the adversary, and will have a different nature and essence from the other two. For the nature of the adversary is corruption and darkness, for he is material and divided into many parts. The nature of the unbegotten Father of everything is incorruption and self-sufficient light, single and uniform. The nature of this God has brought forth two powers . . . he himself however is an image of the higher one. Do not let this disturb you now in your desire to learn how from one beginning of everything, which we confess and believe, unbegotten and incorrupt and good, there came these two natures, one of corruption and one of the middle, both entirely different in nature, though the good one has the ability to beget and bring forth things like itself and of the same nature. For with God's help you will learn in order the beginning and the begetting of this, if you are deemed worthy of the apostolic tradition which we too have received from a succession together with the regulation of all (our) words by the teaching of the Saviour. These matters I have placed before you, my dear sister Flora, in few words, and I have written them as a short summary; yet I have handled the question sufficiently. And it will be highly advantageous to you in the future if through this discussion you will bring forth fruit as a good and fertile land is productive by means of potent seeds." (Epiphanius, *Haer.* xxxiii. 3-7.)

Commentary on the Prologue to the Gospel of John

"John the disciple of the Lord, desiring to describe the generation of all things, makes mention of that Beginning which the Father placed as a foundation, the first-begotten of God, whom he also called 'only-begotten Son' [John iii. 16] and 'God' [John i. 18], in whom the Father created all things seminally. By him the Logos was produced, and in him the whole existence of the aeons, which later the Logos formed. For he speaks thus: 'In the beginning was the Logos, and the Logos was with God, and the Logos was God. The same was in the beginning with God' [John i. 1 *f.*]. In these words distinguishing the three, God, Beginning, and Logos, again he unifies them, in order to show the production of each one, that is, of the Son and the Logos, and their unity with each other and with the Father. For in the Father and from the Father is the Beginning, and from the Beginning the Logos. Rightly he says, 'In the beginning was the Logos,' for he was in the Son. 'And the Logos was with God': for he was the Beginning. 'And the Logos was God': this follows, for what is born of God is God. 'He was in the beginning with God'; this shows the order of production. 'All things were made through him, and apart from him was made nothing' [John i. 3]: for to all the aeons after him the Logos was the author of form and birth. But 'what was made in him was life' [John i. 3 *f.*]. Here it means syzyge, for 'all things' he says 'were made through him,' but life was in him. That which was made in him is doubtless more closely related to him than those things which were made through him; for he exists by himself and bears fruit through himself. Then he says, 'And the life was the light of men' [John i. 4]: by the word 'man' he means the equivalent 'church,' so that through one word he may demonstrate the fellowship of syzyge. For from Logos and Life, Man and Church are born. He calls the Life of men Light because they were lighted by it, that is, formed and made manifest. So also Paul says, 'Everything that is made manifest is light' [Eph. v. 13]. Since, then, the Life begot and made manifest both Man and Church, it is called their Light. Rightly then John makes clear through these words the other, second tetrad, Logos and Life, Man and Church. But also the first tetrad is denoted by this. For speaking about the Saviour and saying that everything outside the Pleroma was formed through him, he says that he himself is the fruit of the whole Pleroma. For he called 'Light' that which 'shines in darkness' and is 'not apprehended' [John i. 5] by it, since forming everything which was made from the passion (of sophia), it (the Light) remained unknown to the darkness. And he calls him Son and Truth and Life and incarnate Logos, 'whose glory we beheld,' he says [John i. 14], and it was his glory as of the only-begotten, given to him by the Father, 'full of grace and truth.' And he says, 'And the Logos became flesh and dwelt among us, and we beheld his glory, glory as of the only-begotten of the Father, full of grace and truth' [John i. 14]. Clearly and accurately then he shows the first tetrad, which he calls Father and Grace and Only-begotten and Truth. Thus John spoke of the first ogdoad, the mother of all the aeons. For he said Father and Grace and Only-begotten and Truth and Logos and Life and Man and Church." (Irenaeus, *Adv. Haer*. i. 8. 5.)

VI.—HERACLEON

Heracleon (about 170) is known to us from his highly
allegorical commentary on John, in which he apparently did
not make use of Ptolemaeus' work. It is the first commentary
on a single gospel known to us, and reveals the high value
placed on John by the Valentinians (see J. N. Sanders, *The
Fourth Gospel in the Early Church*). Apparently, Heracleon
also wrote on Matthew, the other "apostolic" gospel
(fragments 49, 50). He is mentioned by Pseudo-Tertullian
in Section 14.

Commentary on the Gospel of John

1. He limits 'all things' [John i. 3] to "the world and the
things in it. The aeon and the things in the aeon were not
made through the Logos." He joins 'nothing' with "of the
things in the world and the creation. The Logos, who
provided the cause of the creation of the world to the Demiurge, is not the one from whom or by whom but the one
'through' whom. Not as if another were in action did the
Logos make the world (understanding 'through him' thus),
but while he himself was in action another made it." (Origen,
Comm. in Iohann. ii. 14; GCS iv. 70 *ff*. See A. E. Brooke,
Texts and Studies I. 4 [1891].)

2. " 'In him was life' [John i. 4], in spiritual men, for he
provided the first form for them at their birth, carrying
further the things sown by another into form and illumina-
tion and their own outline." (*Ibid.* ii. 21.)

3. [John i. 18] "Spoken not by the Baptist but by the
disciple." (*Ibid.* vi. 3.)

4. [John i. 20 *f.*] "John 'confessed' he was 'not the
Christ,' nor even a 'prophet,' nor 'Elijah.'" (*Ibid.* vi. 15.)

5. [John i. 23] "The Logos is the Saviour; the voice in the
wilderness is that which was represented by John; the sound
is the whole prophetic order. The voice which is well suited

for speech becomes speech, just as if a woman were to change into a man. The Saviour says John is a 'prophet' and 'Elijah'; John denies he is either of these. When the Saviour calls him 'prophet' and 'Elijah' he does not speak of him but of his surroundings. When he calls him a greater than the prophets and than those born of women then he characterizes John. For when John is asked about himself he answers about himself, not about his surroundings. His surroundings were so to speak his apparel, other than himself, and when he was asked about his apparel, as if he himself were his apparel, could he answer Yes?" [John i. 19]. "It was incumbent on such persons, devoted to the service of God, to busy themselves and make inquiries about such matters; furthermore, John was of the Levitical tribe. They asked him if he were a prophet, desiring to know this rather general fact." (*Ibid*. vi. 20 *f*.)

6. [John i. 25] He mentions Christ and Elijah and all the prophets, "whose office alone it is to baptize. The Pharisees put the question from malice, not from a desire to learn." (*Ibid*. vi. 23.)

7. [John i. 26 *f*.] "John answers those sent by the Pharisees, not replying to what they asked, but [saying] what he wanted to." (*Ibid*. vi. 30.)

8. [John i. 26] " 'In the midst of you'; He is already present and is in the world and in man and is already manifest to all of you." [i. 27] "The Baptist confesses through these [words] that he is not worthy of even the least honourable service for Christ. [He means] I am not worthy that for my sake he should come down from greatness and take on flesh as a shoe; concerning this flesh I cannot give a word nor interpret nor explain the economy concerning it. All these things must also be understood concerning that person [the Demiurge] represented by John. The Demiurge of the world, being lesser than Christ, confesses this through

these words. The whole world is the shoe of Jesus." (*Ibid.* vi. 39.)

9. [John i. 28] In Heracleon we read 'Bethany.' [Origen himself read 'Bethabara.'] (*Ibid.* vi. 40.)

10. [John i. 29] " 'Lamb of God' is said by John as a prophet. The first thing is said about his body, the second about him who was in the body; for as the lamb is imperfect among the genus of sheep, so also is the body, compared with him who dwells in it. If he had wanted to indicate by the body that which is perfect he would have said the ram, which was going to be sacrificed." (*Ibid.* vi. 60. See Melito, 10-2.)

11. [John ii. 12] "This again shows the beginning of another economy, since not without significance was 'He went down' spoken; 'Capernaum' signifies the end of the world, those material things to which he went down; and because the place was not suitable he is not said to have done or spoken anything there." (*Ibid.* x. 11.)

12. [John ii. 13] "This is the great feast; for it was a type of the passion of the Saviour, when not only was the sheep slain, but when eaten it afforded rest, and sacrificed signified the passion of the Saviour in the world, and eaten [signified] the rest which is in marriage." (*Ibid.* x. 19 *f.* See Melito, *Homily on the Passion.*)

13. [John ii. 14] "The going up to Jerusalem signifies the journey from mere matter to the stage of living things, which is an image of Jerusalem (above). The words are 'He found in the temple' and not 'in the' court of 'the temple' so that we may understand that the calling without the Spirit is not assisted by the Lord. The 'temple' is the holy of holies, which only the high priest enters (that is, where the spiritual ones go); the court of the temple where the Levites also enter is a symbol of those animal beings who are saved outside the Pleroma. Those who are found 'in the temple

selling oxen and sheep and doves, and the money changers sitting' represent those who attribute nothing to grace but regard the visits of strangers to the temple as a matter of trade and gain, and who minister the sacrifices for the worship of God with a view to their own gain and love of money. And the 'scourge' which Jesus made 'of small cords' is an image of the power and energy of the Holy Spirit, driving out the wicked by his breath. The 'scourge' and the linen and the napkin and other such things are images of the power and energy of the Holy Spirit. The 'scourge' was tied to a piece of wood, which was a type of the cross; on this wood the gamblers, traders, and all evil were nailed up and destroyed. He did not make it of dead leather, for he desired to make the Church no longer a 'den of robbers' and traders, but the house of his Father." (*Ibid*. x. 33.)

14. [John ii. 17] " 'The zeal of thy house shall eat me up' is spoken in the person of those powers which were cast out and destroyed by the Saviour." (*Ibid*. x. 34.)

15. [John ii. 19] Heracleon reads 'in three days' instead of 'on the third day.' He calls the third "the spiritual day, on which is the resurrection of the Church." (For the first is the earthly day and the second the animal, and the resurrection of the Church does not take place on these.) (*Ibid*. x. 37.)

16. [John ii. 20] "Solomon building the temple for forty-six years is an image of the Saviour; the number six refers to matter, that is, what is formed; the forty, which is a tetrad and does not permit combination, refers to the inspiration and the seed in the inspiration." (*Ibid*. x. 38.)

17. [John iv. 14] "That fountain means feeble, short, and deficient life—so too its glory; for it was worldly; it was worldly because from it had drunk the flocks of Jacob. The water which the Saviour gave is from his spirit and his power. 'You shall never thirst': for his life is eternal, and never

corruptible like the first which is from the well, but perma-
nent; for not to be taken away are the grace and the gift of
our Saviour, nor spent or corrupted by him who shares it.
'Springing water': those who accepted the riches supplied
from above themselves poured forth the things supplied to
them, for the eternal life of others. The Samaritan woman
accepted without doubting a faith alien to her nature, not
hesitating over what he said to her. 'Give me this water':
aroused by his short speech she hated even the place of that
so-called living water. These things the woman said to show
the toilsome and laborious and ill-nutritious quality of that
water." (*Ibid.* xiii. 10.)

18. [John iv. 16] "It is clear that this means, If you wish to
receive this water, 'go, call your husband'; the man whom the
Saviour calls the woman's husband is her Pleroma, so that
coming with him to the Saviour she might receive from him
power and union and mixture with her Pleroma; for Christ
did not tell the woman to call her earthly husband, since he
was not unaware that she had no lawful husband. The
Saviour said to her, 'Call your husband and come here',
meaning her companion from the Pleroma. 'Truly you said
that you had no husband,' since in the world the Samaritan
woman had no husband, for her husband was in the Aeon.
The 'six husbands' signify all material evil, to which she
was bound and tied when she fornicated irrationally, and
was insulted and abandoned and slighted by them." (*Ibid.*
xiii. 11.)

19. [John iv. 19] "In proper fashion the Samaritan woman
admitted the things which he said to her; for only a prophet
knows everything. The Samaritan woman acted in accord
with her nature, neither lying nor openly confessing her
immorality. Persuaded that he was a prophet she asked him,
also revealing the cause of her fornication, which was due to
ignorance of God and God's worship and care for the

necessities of life . . . for she would not have come to the well, which was outside the city, unless she had desired to learn in what way and pleasing whom, by the worship of God she might turn away from fornication. Therefore she says 'Our fathers worshipped in this mountain,' etc." (*Ibid*. xiii. 15.)

20. [John iv. 21] "At first Jesus did not say to her, 'Believe me, woman,' but now he addresses her thus. The 'mountain' means the devil, or his world, since the devil was a part of the whole of matter, and the whole world is a mountain of evil, a desert inhabited by wild beasts, which all those under the Law and all the gentiles worship; 'Jerusalem' is the creation or the creator, whom the Jews worship. The 'mountain' is the creation which the gentiles worship; 'Jerusalem' is the creator, whom the Jews adore. But you as spirituals 'will worship' neither the creation nor the Demiurge, but the Father of Truth; and he receives her as already a believer and one counted with those who worship 'in truth'." (*Ibid*. xiii. 16.)

21. [John iv. 22] Heracleon understands 'you' as the Jews. He quotes the Preaching of Peter: "We must not worship in Greek fashion, accepting the works of matter, and adoring wood and stone; nor in Jewish fashion worship the divine, since they, thinking that they alone know him, do not know him, and worship angels and the month and the moon." (*Ibid*. xiii. 17.)

22. [John iv. 22] " 'We worship': The one in the aeon and those who come with him; for these knew the one they worship, worshipping in truth. 'Salvation is of the Jews': because from that race have come salvation and the Logos to the world; in thought salvation is of the Jews, since they are considered images of those beings in the Pleroma." [John iv. 24] " 'In spirit and in truth': Formerly the worshippers worshipped in flesh and error him who is not the the Father, so that they were all in error as worshippers of

the Demiurge. 'They worshipped the creation' and not in truth the creator, who is Christ, since 'All things were made through him and apart from him was not anything made'." (*Ibid*. xiii. 19.)

23. [John iv. 23] "By the abysses of matter and error has been destroyed that [divine element] which is related to the Father; hence the Father seeks to be worshipped by them." He also speaks of the "destruction of the spiritual nature" and the "times or ages before its destruction." (*Ibid*. xiii. 20.)

24. [John iv. 24] " 'God is a Spirit': Undefiled and pure and invisible is his divine nature. 'Worship him in spirit and in truth': Rightly he is worshipped in a spiritual not a carnal manner, for those who are of the same nature as the Father are 'spirit,' who worship in truth and not in error, according to the religion that the Apostle taught, calling it divine service." Some Heracleon says are "fallen; the Samaritan woman, whose nature was spiritual, fornicated." (*Ibid*. xiii. 25.)

25. "The church received Christ, and believed of him that he alone knows all things." (*Ibid*. xiii. 27.)

26. [John iv. 26] "Since the Samaritan woman believed that at Christ's coming he would tell everything to her, he says, Know that I who speak to you am he whom you expect; and when he confessed himself to have come as the expected one, 'his disciples came to him,' and on their account he went into Samaria." (*Ibid*. xiii. 28.)

27. "The waterpot is the condition and thought capable of receiving life and power from the Saviour. They are left behind him, that is, they have such a vessel from the Saviour as that with which she came to take the living water, and went away into the world to proclaim the presence of Christ at his call. For through the Spirit and by the Spirit the soul is drawn to the Saviour." [John iv. 30] " 'They went out of the city': Out of their first way of life, which was worldly, and they came through faith to the Saviour." (*Ibid*. xiii. 31.)

28. "They [the disciples] wanted to share with him what they had bought and brought from Samaria." (*Ibid*. xiii. 32.)

29. 'I have food to eat which you do not know' [John iv. 32]: Heracleon says nothing on this passage. (*Ibid*. xiii. 34.)

30. [John iv. 33] 'Did anyone bring anything for him to eat?' Heracleon takes this carnally of the disciples, "who thinking yet more poorly imitate the Samaritan woman saying 'You have no dipper and the well is deep'." (*Ibid*. xiii. 35.)

31. [John iv. 34] " 'My meat is to do the will of him who sent me': The Saviour explained to the disciples that this which he discussed with the woman was his own food, calling it the 'will' of the Father; for this was his food and rest and power. The 'will' of the Father is for men to know the Father and be saved, which was the Saviour's work, on account of which he was sent into Samaria, that is, into the world." (*Ibid*. xiii. 38.)

32. [John iv. 35 *ff*.] "He speaks of the harvest of the fruits as if this had a fixed period of four months, and were already at hand. The harvest means the souls of believers; they are already ripe and ready for harvest and suitable for gathering into the barn, that is, through faith into rest—some are ready but not all. Some were already ready, but some were about to be; those that are about to be are already sown." (*Ibid*. xiii. 41.)

33. [John iv. 37] " 'One sows, another reaps': This means the same as 'The harvest is great and the workers are few' [Matt. ix. 37], for they are ready for the harvest and suitable for gathering into the barn through faith into rest, and suitable in regard to salvation and the reception of the word, because of their creation and nature." (*Ibid*. xiii. 44.)

34. [John iv. 36] " 'The reaper receives a wage': Since the Saviour calls himself the reaper, the wage of our Lord is the

salvation and restoration of the reaped ones, that he may rest in them." (*Ibid*. xiii. 46.)

35. [John iv. 36] " 'The sower rejoices along with the reaper': For the sower rejoices because he sows, and because some of his seeds have already come together, having the same hope also about the others; and he who reaps likewise reaps something. But the first, who sows, began the work and the second reaps. They cannot both begin at the same time; for first it must be sowed, then it must be reaped. When the sower stops sowing then the reaper reaps. At the present time both having done their own tasks rejoice together, having as a common joy the ripening of the seeds. 'In this the saying is true that one sows, another reaps': For the Son of Man sows over this place, but the Saviour, who is also himself Son of Man, reaps and sends reapers, no doubt those whom the disciples thought were angels, each to his own soul." (*Ibid*. xiii. 49.)

36. [John iv. 36] " 'The sower rejoices with the reaper': Not through them or by them—the apostles—were these seeds sown, but 'those who laboured' are the angels of the economy, through whom as mediators they were sown and nourished. 'You entered into their labours': Not the same is the labour of sowers and of reapers; for the former, in cold and wet and toil ploughing the ground, sow, and throughout the winter care for it by digging; but the latter, entering upon a prepared crop, joyfully reap the harvest." (*Ibid*. xiii. 50.)

37. [John iv. 39] " 'Out of the city': Out of the world. 'Through the word of the woman': For the spiritual church. 'Many': The many who are psychics, for the one nature of election is incorruptible and uniform and unique." (*Ibid*. xiii. 51.)

38. [John iv. 40] "He 'stayed with them' and not in them; and the 'two days': doubtless the present age and the future time of marriage; or the time before his passion and after the

passion, the time which he passed with them, turning many more to faith by his own word, and after which he was separated from them." (*Ibid.* xiii. 52.)

39. [John iv. 42] 'No longer we believe through your word': Heracleon omits the word 'alone'. " 'For we ourselves have heard and we know that he is the Saviour of the world': For men at first believe in the Saviour after being instructed by men; but when they come upon his words, they no longer believe through human testimony alone, but through the truth itself." (*Ibid.* xiii. 53.)

40. [John iv. 46-54, etc.] "The 'king's officer' is the Demiurge, since he is a king over those under him; because his kingdom is small and temporary he was called a minor king, like some petty king appointed by a universal king over a small kingdom. His son in 'Capernaum' is in the lower, intermediate area by the sea, that is, adjoining to matter. The son of this man is sick, that is, is not acting according to nature, but is in ignorance and sins. 'From Judaea to Galilee' means from Judaea above. 'He was going to die' overthrows the opinions of those who suppose the soul is immortal; 'soul and body are destroyed in Gehenna' [Matt. x. 28]. The soul is not immortal but only suited for salvation; the 'corruptible' put on 'incorruption' and the 'mortal' put on 'immortality' when the 'death' of the soul was 'swallowed up in victory' [1 Cor. xv. 54]. 'If you do not see signs and wonders you do not believe' is suitably addressed to such a person as through works and sense-perception has the nature to obey, not through reason the nature to believe. 'Come down before my son dies' means that death is the purpose of Law, which kills through sins. Therefore before he had altogether died on account of his sins, the father asked the Saviour alone to help his son, who was of such a nature. 'Your son lives' the Saviour said through modesty, since he did not say Let him live, nor did he show that he himself

provided life. Going down to the sick man and healing him of the disease, that is, of sins, and by this remission making him alive, he said 'Your son lives.' 'The man believed': The Demiurge can easily believe that even at a distance the Saviour can cure. 'Slaves of the officer' are the angels of the Demiurge, announced in the words 'Your son lives', which is most suitable. Therefore the slaves announced to the officer the things pertaining to the salvation of his son, since the angels first look on the deeds of men in the world to see if they have lived with vigour and genuineness since the sojourn of the Saviour. 'The seventh hour': By the hour he characterizes the nature of the one who was healed. 'He and his whole house believed': This means the angelic order, and men, more closely related to it. It was a question of whether certain angels were saved, those who came down to the 'daughters of men' [Gen. vi. 2]. The destruction of the men of the Demiurge is shown by 'the sons of the kingdom will come into outer darkness' [Matt. viii. 12]. Concerning this Isaiah prophesied: 'I begot sons and raised them up; but they spurned me' [Isaiah i. 2, 4]—they are alien sons and an evil seed and lawless and makers of a vine of thorns" [See Isaiah v. 2]. (*Ibid*. xiii. 60.)

41. [John viii. 12 *ff*.] " 'Where I go you cannot come': How, being in ignorance and unbelief and sins, can they come to be in incorruption?" (*Ibid*. xix. 14.)

42. [John viii. 22] "The Jews thought evilly when they said these things and presumed themselves to be greater than the Saviour, and supposed that they would go to God for eternal rest while the Saviour went to corruption and death, slaying himself, where they did not think they would go. The Jews thought the Saviour said, I having slain myself am going to corruption, where you cannot come." (*Ibid*. xix. 19.)

43. [John viii. 37] " 'My word does not abide in you': For

4

this reason it does not abide, that they are unfit, whether by nature or by inclination." (*Ibid*. xx. 8.)

44. [John viii. 43] "A reason is given for their not 'being able' to 'hear' the words of Jesus, nor know his word, in the 'You are of your father the devil'. Why 'cannot you hear my word'? Is it not that 'You are of your father the devil' means of the nature of the devil? This makes clear to them their nature, and judges them, for they are neither children of Abraham, for they would not have hated him, nor of God, because they did not love him." (*Ibid*. xx. 20.)

45. "Those to whom the word was spoken were of the nature of the devil." (*Ibid*. xx. 23.)

46. [John viii. 44] "The devil does not have will, but desires. . . . These things were spoken, not to the natural earthbound sons of the devil, but to the psychics, who become by choice sons of the devil, from being which by nature some also by choice can become sons of God. By having loved the desires of the devil and doing them these become children of the devil, not being such by nature. In three ways one must bear the name 'children': first by nature, second by inclination, third by merit. By nature, is that which is born from some parent, which is properly called child; by inclination, when someone does someone else's will through his own inclination; by merit, in the way some are called children of Gehenna and darkness and lawlessness, and offspring of snakes and vipers; for these do not beget any offspring according to their own nature, for they are ruinous and wasteful of those who are dashed against them; but since they performed their works they are called their children. . . . Children of the devil he now calls them, not that the devil begets any offspring, but that doing the works of the devil they became like him." (*Ibid*. xx. 24.)

47. [John viii. 44] "For not of truth is his nature, but of the opposite of truth, of deceit and ignorance. Therefore he can

neither stand in the truth nor have truth in him, having falsehood in his own nature, and by nature not being able ever to speak the truth. Not only is he a liar, but so is his father . . . who receives his nature, since he arose from deceit and falsehood." (*Ibid.* xx. 28.)

48. [John viii. 50] "The 'one who seeks and judges' is the one who avenges me, the servant commissioned for this, the one 'not bearing the sword in vain,' the 'avenger' of the king. This is Moses as he prophesied to them saying 'On whom you hoped.' The one who 'judges' and punishes is Moses, who himself is the lawgiver. How then does he say that 'all judgment' was given to him? Rightly he speaks, for the judge doing his will judges as an avenger, just as also it appears to be done among men." (*Ibid.* xx. 38.)

49. [Matt. iii. 11] John said, 'I baptize you with water, but there comes after me he who will baptize you in spirit and fire.' He baptized no one in fire; but some, as Heracleon says, understand by 'fire' the ears of those who are baptized, understanding the apostle's word in this way. (Clement, *Ecl. Proph.* xxv. 1.)

50. [Matt. x. 32-33] "There is one confession which is made by faith and conduct and another by voice. The confession by voice which is made before the authorities is what the many think is the only confession—wrongly; this confession the hypocrites also can make. But this opinion will not be found spoken universally, for not all the saved confessed by their voice and departed—of these are Matthew, Philip, Thomas, Levi, and many others. Confession by the voice is not universal but for a few. But that which he mentions now [Matt. x. 32-3] is universal, *i.e.*, by deeds and actions corresponding to faith in him. This confession is followed by that which is for a few, that before the authorities, if it is necessary and reason requires it. For he will confess with his voice who has rightly confessed first with his

character. And he has well used of those who confess the expression 'in me,' and of those who deny, 'me'. For the latter, though they confess him with the voice, deny him since they do not confess him in their conduct. Only those confess 'in him' who live by their confession and conduct according to him, and 'in them' he also confesses, he who is contained in them and held by them. Therefore he 'never can deny himself' [2 Tim. ii. 13]; but they deny him who are not in him. For he did not say 'Whoever shall deny' in 'me,' but 'me.' For no one who is in him will ever deny him. The expression 'before men' applies both to the saved and similarly to the heathen—by conduct before the former and by voice before the latter." (Clement, *Strom.* iv. 9. 71.)

VII.—MINOR COMMENTATORS

A. Julius Cassianus

Clement of Alexandria calls Cassianus the originator of Docetism, and, like Tatian, a follower of Valentinus. His quotation does not come from a canonical gospel, but from the Gospel according to the Egyptians, whose extant fragments are concerned with a dialogue between Salome and the Lord. Another of Cassianus' works, also known to Clement, was a chronography.

On Continence or *On Castration*

"And let us not say that, since we have members such that thus one is female and another male (one for receiving, the other for sowing), therefore intercourse is from God. For if such an arrangement were from God, to whom we are hastening, he would not have called eunuchs blessed; nor would the prophet have said they 'were not a fruitless tree' [Isaiah lvi. 3], turning from the tree to the man who of his own choice and purpose becomes a eunuch. . . . How wrongly then would one blame the Saviour, if he formed us and freed us from error and from the joining of the members and appendages and genitals. . . . When Salome asked when the things of which he spoke would be known the Lord said, 'When you conceal the garment of shame, and when the two become one, and the male with the female neither male nor female.' " (Clement, *Strom.* iii. 13. 91-2.)

B. Fragment of a Gospel Commentary (?)

Not all Egyptian Christians were "gnostics"; some, like those Jews whose views Philo quotes in his *Quaestiones*, took their sacred books literally. In this second-century papyrus we find the exegesis of a forerunner of that Egyptian bishop Nepos who wrote against allegorists. The underlying question, to be answered by literal interpretation, is "Who are the saved?" Formerly the sacrifices in the temple were efficacious, but now the Lamb of God has been sacrificed. We are reminded of the Epistle to the Hebrews. This fragment is printed by H. I. Bell and T. C. Skeat in *Fragments of an Unknown Gospel and Other Early Christian Papyri* (1935), 42 ff.

1. "It is written, 'The devil takes Jesus to the holy city and set him on the wing of the temple' [Matt. iv. 5]. And again it is written, 'Many bodies of the saints that slept were raised and came into the holy city' [Matt. xxvii. 52-3]."

2. "The Lord saying, 'Blessed are the pure in heart, for they shall see God' [Matt. v. 8]. . . . Of the Dominical Oracles . . . the psalmist . . . 'the oracles of the Lord are pure oracles, fired silver, tested with earth, purified sevenfold' [Ps. xi. 7]."

3. " 'And the Logos became flesh' [John i. 14] . . . after that . . . John . . . but Jesus coming to him, says, 'Behold the Lamb of God that takes away the sin of the world' [John i. 29], showing that . . . coming . . . as it is

written, 'My flesh is food indeed and my blood is drink indeed' [John vi. 55] . . . the true Light . . . he is the beginning, God with God. This is the true Light, a Sun shining above our sun. And to those for whom the Logos, who, being in the form of God, thought it not a prize to be equal to God [Phil. ii. 6], became flesh, to them he is the true Light . . . at the beginnings . . . of three days."

4. "But Paul in the second epistle to Timothy says, 'The Lord knows those who are his' [2 Tim. ii. 19]."

VIII.—PANTAENUS OF ALEXANDRIA

Pantaenus was the earliest teacher of "orthodoxy" at Alexandria; and of his career we know almost nothing; he probably came from Sicily. Since he taught orally and apparently committed nothing to writing, the attempts of various critics to discover his works in other authors are never successful. That there was a catechetical school in his day at Alexandria is rather doubtful. According to tradition he was a missionary in India before settling down as a teacher.

But as I [Origen] was devoted to the word, and the fame of our proficiency was spreading abroad, there approached me, sometimes heretics, sometimes those conversant with Greek learning, and especially philosophy, and I thought it right to examine both the opinions of the heretics, and also the claim that the philosophers make to speak concerning truth. And in doing this we followed the example of Pantaenus, who before us was of assistance to many, and had acquired no small attainments in these matters. (Origen, Epistle in *H.E.* vi. 19. 12 *f.*)

1. 'He set his tabernacle in the sun' [Ps. xix. 4]. Some say, like Hermogenes, that the Saviour himself set his body in the sun; others, the church of the faithful. But our Pantaenus

said, "Usually prophecy makes indefinite statements, and uses the present tense instead of the future, and again the present instead of the past." (Clement, *Ecl. Proph.* 55.)

2. The followers of Pantaenus, being asked in what manner Christians suppose God to know reality, replied, "He neither knows sensible things by sense, nor intelligible things by intellect. For it is not possible that he who is above the things that exist should apprehend the things that exist according to the things that exist. We say that he knows the things that exist as acts of his own will." (Maximus, *Schol. in Greg. Naz.*; Routh, *Rel. Sacr.* i. 379.)

SYRIAN CHRISTIANITY

IX.—ARISTO OF PELLA

Of Aristo we know nothing not presented in these fragments. The loss of his *Disputation* is the more regrettable in that it probably presented a conservative Hebrew Christian's arguments against a liberal Alexandrian Jew. Origen describes it thus: "In this book a Christian is described as arguing with a Jew from the Jewish scriptures, and showing that the prophecies concerning the Messiah refer to Jesus; and yet the adversary resists vigorously and in conformity with his Jewish character" (*Contra Celsum* iv. 52). A later preface to the lost work says: "That famous, memorable and glorious thing takes place, the dispute of Jason the Hebrew Christian and Papiscus the Alexandrine Jew: the obstinate hardness of the Jewish heart is softened by the Hebrew advice and gentle chiding; victorious in the heart of Papiscus is Jason's doctrine of the infusion of the Holy Spirit. How Papiscus was admitted to the understanding of the truth, and disposed to the fear of the Lord when the Lord himself took pity, and believed in Jesus Christ the Son of God, and how he besought Jason that he might take on the sign [of the cross]. The writing of their debate (in Greek) proves this: they contend, Papiscus opposing the truth and Jason asserting and vindicating the disposition and fullness of Christ." (Celsus' [?] Preface; Routh, *Rel. Sacr.* i. 97.)

1. "The war was at its height in the eighteenth year of the rule [of Hadrian], round about Beth-ther, a small but very strong town not very far from Jerusalem, where a protracted siege brought the revolutionaries to complete destruction through hunger and thirst, and the author [Bar Cochba] of their folly paid the just penalty. From that time forward the whole nation was wholly prohibited from setting foot upon the country round about Jerusalem, by the decree and ordin-

ances of a law of Hadrian, which forbade them to gaze, even from afar, on the soil inherited from their fathers." (*H.E.* iv. 6. 3.)

Disputation of Jason and Papiscus

2. "The curse of God is he who is hung." (Jerome, *Comm. in Gal.* ii. 3. 13; Routh i. 95.)

3. "In the Son God made heaven and earth." (Jerome, *Quaest. in Gen.* ii.; Routh i. 95.)

4. "Seven heavens." (Maximus, *Schol. in Dion. Areop.* i.; Routh i. 96.)

X.—HEGESIPPUS

The work of Hegesippus seems to have been a collection of legends about the apostles and their contemporaries. His theory of church history was that the Church remained a "pure virgin" in the apostles' day (until the reign of Trajan) and was then corrupted by heresies. To these legends Hegesippus added information about later affairs, such as the cultus of Hadrian's favourite Antinous (Frag. 7) and the succession of bishops at Rome (Frag. 8). It is possible that Fragment 9 has been mistakenly attributed to him, though any second-century chiliast might have written it.

He states some particulars from the Gospel of the Hebrews and from the Syriac, and especially from the Hebrew language, showing that he himself was a convert from the Hebrews. Other matters he also records as taken from the unwritten tradition of the Jews. And not only he, but also Irenaeus and the whole chorus of the ancients, called the Proverbs of Solomon all-virtuous Wisdom. And in speaking of the so-called apocryphal books, he tells that some of them were forged in his own times by some of the heretics. (*H.E.* iv. 22. 8.)

1. "The various opinions in the circumcision among the

sons of the Israelites against the tribe of Judah and the Messiah were these: Essenes, Galileans, Hemerobaptists, Masbotheans, Samaritans, Sadducees, and Pharisees." (*H.E.* iv. 22. 7.)

2. (*Book V*) "With the apostles James the brother of the Lord received the succession in the church. He was called the Just by everyone from the Lord's times up to our own, since many were called James. But he was holy from his mother's womb; he did not drink wine or fermented drink, nor did he eat anything in which was life. No razor passed over his head, he never anointed himself with oil, and he did not use the bath. It was lawful for him alone to enter into the Holy of Holies, for he did not wear wool but linen. Alone he entered into the temple, and was found kneeling on his knees and seeking forgiveness for the people, so that his knees grew hard as a camel's because he was always kneeling on them, worshipping God and asking forgiveness for the people. Because of the greatness of his righteousness he was called Just and Obdias* (that is in Greek 'Protection of the people' and 'Righteousness'), as the prophets foretold of him. Then certain of the seven heresies (mentioned before) among the people asked him: What is the teaching [Torah?] of Jesus? And he said: That he is Saviour. Some of them believed that Jesus is the Messiah. The heresies previously mentioned do not believe either in his resurrection or in his coming to reward each according to his works; but as many as believed did so on James' account. Then when many of the rulers also believed, there was a disturbance of the Jews and scribes and Pharisees, saying that the whole people is in danger of expecting Jesus as Messiah. Then coming to James they said: 'We urge you to restrain the people, since they are led astray to Jesus as if he were the Messiah. We

---

* Emending the text with C. C. Torrey in *Journal of Biblical Literature* 63 (1944), 93 ff. (1 Kings xviii. 3 ff.). Text: Oblias.

urge you to persuade all those who come for the day of
Passover about Jesus; for we all trust you. We and all the
people bear witness to you that you are just and not a
respecter of persons. Therefore persuade the crowd not to
be led astray concerning Jesus; for we and all the people
trust you. Stand on the pinnacle of the temple, so that you
can be seen from on high and your words can be clearly
audible to the whole people. For because of the Passover
all the tribes have come and the gentiles too.' Then the
previously mentioned scribes and Pharisees set James on the
pinnacle of the temple and shouted to him and said: 'Justus,
we all ought to trust you. Since the people are being led
astray after Jesus the crucified, tell us what the teaching of
Jesus is.' And he answered in a loud voice: 'Why do you ask
me about the Son of Man, when he sits in heaven on the
right hand of the Great Power, and is coming on the clouds
of heaven?' And when many were persuaded and gloried in
the testimony of James and said, 'Hosanna to the Son of
David,' then again the same scribes and Pharisees said to one
another: 'We did wrong in allowing such a testimony to
Jesus; but let us go up and throw him down, so that they
will be afraid to believe in him.' And they shouted: 'Oh, oh!
Justus himself is deceived.' And they fulfilled the scripture,
written in Isaiah: 'Let us take away the just man, for he is
offensive to us; wherefore they shall eat the fruits of their
doings.' Then they went up and threw Justus down. And
they said to one another: 'Let us stone James the Just.' And
they began to stone him, since he did not die when he was
thrown down. But he turned and knelt down and said: 'I
exhort thee, Lord God, Father, forgive them, for they know
not what they do.' As they were stoning him thus, one of the
priests of the sons of Rechab (the son of Rechabim), spoken of
by Jeremiah the prophet, cried out and said: 'Stop! What
are you doing? Justus is praying for you!' And one of them,

a fuller, took a club which he used to beat clothes and smashed it against the head of Justus, and so he was martyred. And they buried him on the spot by the temple, and there his monument still lies, by the temple. He became a true witness both to Jews and to Greeks that Jesus is the Messiah. And at once Vespasian attacked them." (*H.E.* ii. 23. 4-18.)

3. "And after James the Just was martyred as the Lord was, for the same offence, Simeon the son of Klopas the Lord's uncle was appointed bishop, a man whom everyone approved of, since he was a cousin of the Lord, as the second [bishop]. For this reason they called the church a virgin, for she had not yet been corrupted by vain discourses; but Thebouthis, because he had not become a bishop, began to corrupt her from the seven heresies among the people, to which he himself belonged. From these also came Simon, whence the Simonians, and Cleobius, whence the Cleobians, and Dositheus, whence the Dositheans, and Gorthaeus, whence the Gorathenes [and Masbotheans]. From these the Menandrianists and Marcionites and Carpocratians and Valentinians and Basilidians and Saturnilians have introduced their own opinions in different ways; from these have come false Christs, false prophets, false apostles, who have divided the unity of the church with corrupting words against God and against his Christ." (*H.E.* iv. 22. 4.)

4. "Some of these heretics accused Simeon the son of Klopas of being a descendant of David, and a Christian; and so he was martyred, being 120 years old, under Trajan and the legate Atticus." (*H.E.* iii. 32. 3.)

4. "They came then, and took the lead in the whole church as witnesses and relatives of the Lord, and, since there was profound peace in the whole church, they survived until the emperor Trajan, until the son of an uncle of the Lord, the previously mentioned Simeon son of Klopas, falsely accused by the sects, was similarly accused on the

same charge before the legate Atticus. And after being tortured many days he bore witness, so that all were amazed, even the legate, at how he endured, being 120 years old. Finally, he was ordered off to be crucified." (The same man, relating the events of the times, says that the church continued until then as a pure and uncorrupt virgin. If there were any who tried to corrupt the sound doctrine of the preaching of salvation, they still hid in a dark hiding place. But when the sacred chorus of the apostles in various ways departed from life, as well as the generation of those who were deemed worthy to hear their inspired wisdom, then also the faction of godless error arose by the deceit of teachers of another doctrine. These, since none of the apostles survived, henceforth attempted shamelessly to preach their 'knowledge falsely so-called' [1 Tim. vi. 20] against the preaching of the truth). (*H.E.* iii. 32. 7 *f*.)

6. "There were still living from the family of the Lord the grandsons of Judas, called his brother after the flesh; these were informed against as being of the family of David. The evocatus brought them to Domitian Caesar. For he feared the coming of Christ as did Herod. And he asked them if they were of David's family, and they admitted it. Then he asked them what possessions they had or how much money they owned. They said that between them they had nine thousand denarii, half of which belonged to each of them; and this, they said, was not in silver, but in the value of only thirty-nine plethra of land, on which by their labour they paid taxes and supported themselves. Then they showed him their hands as evidence of the hardness of their bodies and the callouses on their hands formed by incessant work, as proof of their labour. And when they were asked about the Christ and his kingdom, what it is and where and when it would appear, they replied that it was not worldly or earthly, but heavenly and angelic, appearing at the end of the

age, when he would come in glory to judge the living and the dead and to give to each according to his merits. For these remarks Domitian did not condemn them, but despising them as fools sent them away free, and through a decree stopped the persecution of the church. After they were set free they directed the churches both as witnesses and as relatives of the Lord. And since there was peace, they remained alive until the reign of Trajan." (*H.E.* iii. 20. 1.)

7. "To whom they erected cenotaphs and temples, as we see to this day. Among them was Antinous, the slave of the emperor Hadrian, in whose honour games are celebrated too; he lived in our own times. For he also founded a city named after Antinous, and instituted prophets." (*H.E.* iv. 8. 2.)

8. (After some observations on the epistle of Clement to the Corinthians) "And the church of Corinth remained in the true faith until Primus was bishop in Corinth; I lived with them on my way to Rome and stayed with them many days, during which we were refreshed with the true teaching. And when I was in Rome I made a list of bishops up to Anicetus; Eleutherus was his deacon; Soter succeeded to Anicetus. After him came Eleutherus. In each succession and in each city things are done just as the Law, the prophets, and the Lord preach." (*H.E.* iv. 22. 2 *f.*)

9. " 'The good things prepared for the just, eye saw not, and ear heard not, nor did they enter into the heart of man' [1 Cor. ii. 9]. These things were spoken vainly, and those who said them lied against the divine scriptures and the Lord, who said: 'Blessed are your eyes which see and your ears which hear,' etc. [Matt. xiii. 16]." (Steph. Gob. in Photius, 232.)

XI.—SERAPION, BISHOP OF ANTIOCH

Serapion was bishop of Antioch at the end of the second century, and was a strong anti-Montanist. On a visit to the nearby town of Rhossus he was asked by some members of the church to allow the liturgical reading of the Gospel of Peter. Merely glancing at it, the bishop gave his permission. On his return to Antioch he was informed of its heretical nature, and, after obtaining a copy from Antiochene docetists, he wrote this letter setting forth the heretical elements in the gospel. Of Serapion's other writings Eusebius knew only his work addressed to Domnus, one who had become a Jewish proselyte during "the persecution"—doubtless under Septimus Severus (soon after 199).

To Caricus and Pontius

1. "But that you may also know this, that the work of this lying party of the so-called New Prophecy is abominated by the whole brotherhood in the world, I have sent you also a letter of Claudius Apollinaris, who was the most blessed bishop in Hierapolis in Asia." In this epistle of Serapion are extant the signatures of various bishops, one of whom signed thus: "I, Aurelius Quirinus, a witness, pray that you may be well." Another, in this fashion: "Aelius Publius Julius, a bishop from Debeltum a colony in Thrace. As God in heaven lives, I swear that the blessed Sotas of Anchialus wanted to cast out Priscilla's demon, and the hypocrites would not let him." And the autograph signatures of a large number of other bishops, agreeing with these, are extant in the said letter. (*H.E.* v. 19.)

On the So-called Gospel of Peter

2. "We, brethren, receive both Peter and the other apostles as Christ, but the writings which falsely go under their names we reject, being experienced and knowing that

such were not handed down to us. For when I was among you, I supposed that all of you held to the true faith, and not having gone through the Gospel presented by them under the name of Peter, I said: If this is the only thing that seems to cause faultfinding among you, let it be read. But since I have now learned, from what has been told me, that their mind was enveloped in some heresy, I will make haste to come to you again; therefore, brethren, expect me quickly. But we, brethren, understanding to what heresy Marcianus belonged (who used to contradict himself, not knowing what he said, as you will learn from what has been written to you)—were enabled by others who studied this same Gospel, that is, by the successors of those who began it, whom we call Docetists (for most of the ideas belong to their teaching)—using [information given] by them we were enabled to go through it and find that most was of the Saviour's true teaching, but that some things were added, which we list below for you."
(*H.E.* vi. 12. 3-6.)

ASIATIC CHRISTIANITY

XII.—PAPIAS, BISHOP OF HIERAPOLIS

Papias was bishop of Hierapolis in Phrygia early in the second century. He collected traditional materials in order to illustrate the Dominical Oracles, which were probably the four gospels and the Apocalypse. The first fragment shows his preference for the "living voice" as a source of exegesis. He asked followers of the elders (disciples of the Lord) what the elders had said, and in a special case he asked what Aristion and the elder John had said. Whether with Eusebius we should distinguish between the two disciples named John mentioned here is entirely uncertain. Papias' teaching is more in harmony with the Apocalypse than with the gospel of John; yet he quotes the teaching of the Johannine gospel to illustrate a verse from Matthew (frag. 8). He seems also to have provided exegesis for part of the book of Genesis, but of it little is known.

Exegesis of the Dominical Oracles

Prologue

1. "I will not hesitate to set down in writing for you whatever I used to learn well from the elders and well remembered, maintaining the truth about them. For not like the many did I enjoy those who spoke the most, but those who taught the truth, not those who recalled the commands of others, but those who delivered the commands given by the Lord to faith and (coming) from the truth itself. But if by chance anyone came who had followed the elders, I inquired about the words of the elders: what Andrew or Peter said, or what Philip, or Thomas or James, or John or Matthew or any other of the Lord's disciples, or what Aristion and the elder John, the Lord's disciples, said. For I did not suppose that things

from books would help me as much as things from a living
and surviving voice." (*H.E.* iii. 39. 4.)

Book I

2. "The first Christians called those who studied purity
before God by the name of children." (Maximus, *Schol. in
Dion. Areop.* ii.; Routh, *Rel. Sacr.* i. 8.)

Book II

3. Papias relates in his second book of the Dominical
Oracles that John was slain by the Jews, fulfilling manifestly,
together with his brother, the prediction of Christ concerning them, and their own confession and undertaking in the
matter. (Georgius Hamartolos; *cf.* E. Preuschen, *Anti-
legomena* [ed. 1] 58.)

Book IV

4. "There will be enjoyment of foods in the resurrection."
(Maximus, *Schol. in Dion. Areop.* vii.; Preuschen, 61.)

5. "The days will come, when vines will grow up, each
having ten thousand shoots, and in one shoot ten thousand
branches, and in one branch ten thousand vine-shoots, and
in each vine-shoot ten thousand clusters, and in each cluster
ten thousand grapes; and each grape when pressed will give
twenty-five measures of wine. And when anyone takes one of
those holy vine-shoots, another will shout, 'I am a better
vine-shoot; take me; bless the Lord through me.' Likewise
a grain of wheat will bring forth ten thousand ears, and each
ear will have ten thousand grains, and each grain, five two-
pound measures of excellent fine flour; and the rest of the
fruits and seeds and herb in harmony follow them; and all
the animals, using those foods which are received from the
earth, become peaceful and in harmony with one another,
being subject to men in complete submission. These things

are credible to believers. And Judas the traitor, who did not believe, asked: 'How, then, will such creatures be brought to perfection by the Lord?' The Lord said, 'They who come in them will see.' " (Irenaeus, *Adv. Haer.* v. 33. 3, 4; *cf.* Hippolytus, *Comm. in Dan.* iv. 60.)

6. "A great example of impiety was Judas walking about in the world. His flesh was so bloated that wherever a wagon could easily pass through, he could not, not even with his swollen head. For his eyelids were so swollen that he could not see light at all. His eyes could not be made visible even by a surgeon's knife. Such was his decline as to his external appearance. His genitals seemed the most unpleasant and greatest part of his whole disfigurement, and it was said that from his whole body flowed pus and worms with violence caused by their own force alone. After many torments and punishments he died on his own property; and because of the smell the spot is deserted and uninhabited even now. But no one can go to that place to this day unless he stops his nostrils with his hands; so great a discharge took place through his flesh and on the land." (Cramer, *Catena*, on Acts i. 18; vol. iii, p. 12; Preuschen, 62.)

Book IV (?)

7. Papias, their contemporary, mentions that he had a wonderful story from the daughters of Philip. For he relates that the resurrection of a dead body took place in his day; and, on the other hand, he tells of another miraculous happening, concerned with Justus who was surnamed Barsabbas: that he drank a deadly poison and by the grace of the Lord suffered no unpleasant effects. . . . And the same writer has quoted other things also as coming to him from unwritten tradition; for instance, certain strange parables of the Saviour and teachings of his, and some other things of a rather mythical character. And among these is his statement

that there will be a certain period of a thousand years after the resurrection of the dead, when the kingdom of Christ will be set up in a material order on the earth. (*H.E.* iii. 39. 9-12.)

8. "Those who are worthy of life in heaven will go there; others will enjoy the delights of paradise; others will possess the brightness of the city; for everywhere the Lord will be seen, as those who see him are worthy. There is this distinction between those who bring forth fruit a hundredfold and sixtyfold and thirtyfold [Matt. xiii. 23]; the first will be taken up into heaven, the second will live in paradise, and the third will inhabit the city. For this reason the Lord said, 'In my Father's [house] are many mansions' [John xiv. 2]. For all things are God's, and he provides a suitable dwelling for everyone." (Irenaeus, *Adv. Haer.* v. 36. 1, 2.)

9. "To some of them [the angels] he gave charge over the affairs of the earth, and he ordered them to rule well. . . . But their order ended in nothing." (Andr. Caes. *in Apoc.* 34, 12; Routh, *Rel. Sacr.* i. 14.)

10. [Papias and others] understand the whole six days' work [of creation] in reference to Christ and the church. (Anastasius Sinaiticus, *Contemp. anag. in Hex.* i. [Routh, i. 15].)

11. [Papias and others] refer the things concerning paradise to the church of Christ. (Anastasius Sinaiticus, *Contemp. anag. in Hex.* vii. [Routh, i. 15].)

Prologue (?)

12. "This also the elder used to say. Mark, indeed, having been the interpreter of Peter, wrote accurately, though not in order, all that he recalled of what was either said or done by the Lord. For he neither heard the Lord, nor was he a follower of his, but at a later date (as I said) of Peter; who used to adapt his instructions to the needs [of the

moment], but not with a view to putting together the Dominical oracles in orderly fashion: so that Mark did no wrong in thus writing some things as he recalled them. For he kept a single aim in view: not to omit anything of what he heard, nor to state anything therein falsely." (*H.E.* iii. 39. 15.)

13. "Matthew then compiled the oracles in the Hebrew language; but everyone interpreted them as he was able." (*H.E.* iii. 39. 16.)

XIII.—MELITO, BISHOP OF SARDIS

Melito, a Quartodeciman bishop of Sardis about 170, was one of the most voluminous writers of his century; but only his Homily on the Passion (edited by Campbell Bonner in 1940) has survived in a fairly complete form. Like the earlier "Barnabas" Melito was an ardent student of "typology," the means whereby Christ was read into the Old Testament. Many of his fragments are preserved only in Syriac, and may have been composed in that language. Polycrates' reference (XVI) to him as a eunuch probably means no more than that he lived as a celibate. Eusebius lists his works as follows: "Two books On the Passover; On the Conduct of Life and the Prophets; On the Church; On the Lord's Day; further On the Faith of Man; On Creation; On the Subjection of the senses to Faith; besides these On the Unity of Soul and Body; On Baptism; On Truth; On Faith; On the Birth of Christ; On the Prophetic Word; On Soul and Body; On Hospitality; The Keys; On the Devil and the Apocalypse of John; On the Corporeality of God; last of all, the book To Antoninus." (To these should be added the Eclogues and the Homily on the Passion.) (*H.E.* iv. 26. 2.)

To Antoninus

1. "For—a thing that never happened before—the race of the pious is persecuted, harassed by new decrees throughout Asia. For shameless informers and lovers of others' goods, taking advantage of the decrees, openly plunder us, night

and day robbing innocent persons. And if this is done by your order, let it be done properly. For a just king should never deliberate unjustly. We, indeed, gladly accept the honour of such a death; but we ask only this favour of you —that you yourself, first taking note of the workers of such contention, justly judge whether they are worthy of death and punishment or safety and security. But if this decision, and this new ordinance, which is not proper even against hostile barbarians, are not from you, all the more we beg you not to overlook us in such a public persecution. For our philosophy at first flourished among barbarians, but after appearing among your peoples during the powerful rule of your ancestor Augustus it became a blessing especially to your empire. For at that time the might of the Romans increased to something great and splendid; you, hoped for by men, have become its successor, and will continue, along with your son, if you protect the philosophy which was cradled and took its beginning with Augustus, and which your ancestors honoured along with the other cults. This is the greatest proof that our teaching flourished for the good along with the empire as it happily started out: from the time of Augustus nothing evil has befallen it, but on the contrary everything has been splendid and praiseworthy in accordance with the prayers of all. Alone of all, persuaded by certain malignant persons, Nero and Domitian wanted to bring our teaching into ill repute; and since their time by an unreasonable custom false information about such people has become common. But your godly fathers corrected their ignorance, many times rebuking in writing those many persons who had dared to make disturbances about them. Among these was your grandfather Hadrian, who wrote to the proconsul Fundanus, governor of Asia, and many others; and your father, when you were ruling the world with him, wrote to the cities—among others to the Larissians and the

Thessalonians and the Athenians and all the Greeks—not to make disturbances concerning us. But since you have the same opinion on these matters as they did, and a much greater love of mankind and of wisdom, we are the more persuaded that you will do everything we ask." (*H.E.* iv. 26. 5-11.)

2. "We are not servants of stones which have no feeling, but we are worshippers of the only God, who is before all and above all, and of his Christ, who is the Word of God before all ages." (*Chron. pasch.* p. 483, Dindorf [Otto-Goodspeed, 2].)

Selections

3. "Melito to his brother Onesimus, greeting. Since you often requested, in your zeal for the word, to have selections from the Law and the Prophets concerning the Saviour and our faith as a whole; and moreover you wanted to learn the exact truth concerning the ancient books, in regard to their number and their order; I was zealous to perform such a task, knowing your zeal for the faith and love for the study of the word, and that you, in your yearning for God, esteem these things above everything else, contending for the prize of eternal salvation. Therefore, having gone up to the East and come to the place where these things were proclaimed and done, and having exactly learned which the books of the Old Covenant are, I am sending you the list of them which is given below. These are their names. Of Moses, five books: Genesis, Exodus, Numbers, Leviticus, Deuteronomy; Jesus Nave, Judges, Ruth; four of Kings, two of Chronicles; Psalms of David; of Solomon, Proverbs (also called Wisdom), Ecclesiastes, Song of Songs; Job; of prophets, [the books of] Isaiah, Jeremiah, the twelve in a single roll, Daniel, Ezekiel; Esdras. From these I have made the selections (eclogues), dividing them into six books." (*H.E.* iv. 26. 13 *f.*)

Eclogues (?)

4. "He was bound as a ram and shorn as a lamb, and as a sheep was led to the sacrifice and as a lamb was crucified, and he bore the wood on his shoulders, being led up to be sacrificed like Isaac by his Father. But Christ suffered, while Isaac did not suffer; for *he* was a type of Christ who was going to suffer. But he being the type of Christ caused stupor and fear to men. For it was a new mystery to see a son led by his father to a mountain for sacrifice, whom having bound he placed on the logs to be consumed, preparing with haste the things for his sacrifice. But Isaac is silent, bound as a ram, not opening his mouth or speaking with his voice. For, not fearing the sword, nor trembling at the fire, nor grieving at suffering, he bore patiently the type of the Lord. Then Isaac was set forth in the midst bound as a ram, and Abraham standing by and holding the naked sword, not ashamed to slay his son." (Otto, Goodspeed, 9.)

5. "On behalf of the just Isaac a lamb appeared for the sacrifice, that Isaac might be loosed from his bonds. Being sacrificed it redeemed Isaac; so also the Lord being sacrificed saved us and being bound loosed us and being sacrificed redeemed us." (Otto, Goodspeed, 10.)

6. "For the Lord was the lamb as the ram which Abraham saw caught in the bush of Sabec; but the bush set forth the cross and that place set forth Jerusalem, and the Lamb, the Lord entangled for the sacrifice." (Otto, Goodspeed, 11.)

On the Passover

7. "In the time of Servilius Paulus, proconsul of Asia, at the time when Sagaris was martyred, there was much dispute in Laodicea about the Passover, which in those days fell at the (right ?) time, and these things were written." (Otto, Goodspeed, 4.)

On the Devil and the Apocalypse of John

8. Melito who was in Asia says that he [Absalom] was a type of the devil resisting Christ's kingdom, and making mention only of this he does not expound the passage extensively. (Otto, Goodspeed, 5.)

On the Incarnation of Christ, Book III

9. "There is no need, for those who are intelligent, to prove the real and substantial nature of his soul and body—that nature human like ourselves—out of the things which Christ did after his baptism. For the things done after the baptism by Christ, and especially the signs, made clear the divinity hidden in his flesh, and confirmed it to the world. For being at the same time God and perfect man he confirmed his two natures to us, his divinity through the signs in the three years after his baptism, his humanity in the thirty years before the baptism, in which because of his imperfection according to the flesh he hid the signs of his divinity, though he was true God before the ages." (Otto, Goodspeed, 6.)

On Baptism

10. "Are not gold and silver and copper and iron, after being fired, baptized with water? The one that its surface may be cleansed, the other that through dipping it may be made strong. The whole earth is washed with rains and rivers, and when it is washed is excellently cultivated. Just so, the land of Egypt, washed by the overflow of the river, increases its crop, makes the ear of corn full, and is farmed a hundredfold—because of its good baptism. And even the air itself is washed by the downfall of the showers. The blossoming mother of rains, Iris, is washed too, whenever at the time of flowing rains she fills the rivers, invoked by a water-leading spirit. If you wish to consider the heavens as

baptized, turn now to the ocean and there I will show you a new sight: the open sea and the limitless sea and the boundless deep and the immeasurable ocean and the pure water, the baptistery of the sun and the lamp-lighting place for the stars and the bath of the moon; now how in a mystery they are washed you may learn in faith from me. The sun, accomplishing the day's course with his fiery steeds, becomes fiery in the whirling of his course and is lighted like a lamp, burning up the middle zone of his course. As he appears near with ten lightning rays he beats the earth, and goes importunate into the ocean. As a copper globe, full of fire within, flashing much light, is washed in cold water with a great noise, but the fire within is not quenched but again flashes fierily—so the sun, burning like lightning, is washed wholly but not extinguished in cold water, having its fire unquenched; washed in a mystic baptism he rejoices exceedingly, having the water for nourishment; for remaining one and the same he rises as a new sun to men, made strong from the deep, purified from the baptism, driving out the darkness of night, he begat the light of day. On this course also the movement of the stars and of the moon by nature moves; for they are washed at the baptistery of the sun, like good disciples; for the stars with the moon follow in the path of the sun, having pure sunlight. Now if the sun with the stars and moon is washed in the ocean, why is Christ not washed in the Jordan? King of heaven and governor of creation, sun of the east, who also appeared to the dead in Hades and the mortals in the world, and, the only sun, shone forth from heaven." (Pitra, *Analecta Sacra* ii. 3-5 [Goodspeed, 8].)

On Soul and Body

11. "Therefore God, desiring to visit his creation which he had made in his own image and likeness, in the last times sent his incorporeal and only Son into the world, who,

becoming incarnate in the virgin's womb, was born a perfect man that he might save lost man, collecting his scattered members. For otherwise why did Christ have to die? Was he guilty unto death? When he was God, why did he become man? Why did he come down to earth, he who reigned in heaven? Who forced God to come down to earth, to take on flesh from the holy virgin, to be rolled up in swaddling clothes in a stable, to be nourished with milk, to be baptized in the Jordan, to be mocked by the people, to be fastened to the tree, to be buried in the ground, to rise from the dead on the third day, giving his life for life for the sake of redemption, blood for blood, undergoing death for death? For Christ dying paid the debt of death to which man was subject. O new and unspeakable mystery! the judge was judged; he who loosed from sins was bound; he was mocked who had made the world; he was stretched out on the cross who stretched out the heavens; he was nourished with gall who supplied manna in place of food; he was handed over to the tomb who raises the dead. The virtues were amazed, the angels marvelled, the elements trembled, every created thing was shaken, the light of day withdrew; for they could not bear to see their Lord crucified. The astonished creation said: What is this new mystery? The judge is judged, and is silent; the invisible one is seen, and is not ashamed; the incomprehensible one is comprehended, and is not indignant; the immeasurable one is held in a measure, and does not struggle; the impassible one suffers, and does not take vengeance; the deathless one dies, and does not complain; the heavenly one is buried, and bears it with calm mind. Of what sort, I say, is this mystery? Certainly the creation is astounded. When however the Lord rose from death and trod on it, when he bound the strong and freed man, then every creature after Adam marvelled that the judge was judged, the invisible visible, the impassible suffering, the undying dead, the heavenly buried in the earth. For the Lord became man; he was condemned that he might obtain mercy; he was bound that he might loose; he was caught that he might free; he suffered that he might heal our sufferings; he died that he might give us life; he was buried that he might raise us. For when the Lord suffered his humanity suffered, which he possessed like man; and he who was like man loosed his passions; and dying he destroyed death. For this reason he came down to earth, that undergoing death he might slay the rebellious slayer of men. For one submitted to judgement—thousands were freed; one was buried—thousands rose. He is the mediator between God and men; he is the resurrection and salvation of all; he is the leader of the lost, the shepherd of freed men, the life of the dead, the charioteer of the cherubim, the leader of the angels, and the king of kings. To whom be glory for ever. Amen." (A. Mai, *Nova Patrum bibliotheca* ii. 539; Otto, 13.)

On the Cross

12. "For this he came to us, for this, though he was incorporeal, he formed a body for himself from our shape. He who seemed a lamb remained a shepherd; he who was considered a slave did not deny the exalted position of a son; borne of Mary and made by his Father; treading on earth and filling heaven; appearing as a boy and not concealing the eternity of his nature; he appeared a poor man and did not deprive himself of his riches; insofar as he was man, in need of food, insofar as he was God, not failing to feed the world; he put on the appearance of a slave and did not change the appearance of his Father. His nature was always changeless. He stood before Pilate and he sat with the Father; he was fastened to the tree and he held the world." (Otto, 14.)

On Faith

13. "From the Law and the Prophets we have collected the prophecies concerning our Lord Jesus Christ, that we may prove to your love that he is perfect reason, the Logos of God; who was begotten before light; who was creator of all with the Father; who was the fashioner of men; who was all in all: who was a patriarch of patriarchs, law of law, high priest of priests, governor of kings, prophet of prophets, archangel of angels, the Word of voices, the Spirit of spirits, Son of the Father, God of God, King forever. He was Noah's pilot, he led Abraham, he was bound with Isaac, he was Jacob's fellow-traveller, he was sold with Joseph, he was a leader with Moses, he distributed the inheritance with Joshua the son of Nun, he foretold his sufferings through David and the prophets: who was incarnate in the virgin, who was born at Bethlehem, who was wrapped up in swaddling clothes in a stable, who was seen by the shepherds, who was praised by the angels, who was adored by the magi, who was announced by John, who gathered the apostles, who preached the kingdom, who cured the lame, who gave light to the blind, who raised the dead, who was seen in the temple, who was not believed by the people, who was betrayed by Judas, who was arrested by the priests, who was judged by Pilate, who was fixed with a spear in his flesh, who was suspended on the tree, who was buried in the earth, who rose from the dead, who appeared to the apostles, who was taken up into heaven, who sits at the right hand of the Father, who is the rest of the dead, the finder of the lost, the light of those who are in darkness, the redeemer of the captives, the guide of wanderers, the refuge of those who mourn, the spouse of the Church, the charioteer of the cherubim, the chief of the army of angels, God of God, Son of the Father, Jesus Christ, King for ever. Amen." (Otto, 15.)

XIV.—CLAUDIUS APOLLINARIS, BISHOP OF HIERAPOLIS

Claudius Apollinaris was bishop of Hierapolis in Asia Minor, the city where Papias had lived, in the last third of the second century. He was probably on the Quartodeciman side in the Easter controversy; note his third fragment, which may be based on a passage in Melito's Homily on the Passion. The reason Polycrates (XVI) does not mention him is that he is listing only the relatives of John. Serapion (XI) mentions him as a noted anti-Montanist writer.

While there are many works of Apollinaris preserved by many, those which have come to us are these: a speech to the above-mentioned emperor (Marcus Aurelius) and five books —*Against the Greeks*, and *Concerning Truth I and II*, and *Against the Jews I and II*, and the ones which he wrote after these *Against the Heresy of the Phrygians*. (*H.E.* iv. 27.)

1. "From that time the legion which through prayer had performed this miracle received from the Emperor a name suited to the deed, being called 'thundering' in the Roman tongue." (*H.E.* v. 5. 4.)

2. (*Concerning the Passover*) "There are some who through ignorance are contentious about these things, suffering for a pardonable offence; for ignorance does not receive accusation, but needs instruction. And they say that on the fourteenth day the Lord ate the lamb with his disciples, but on the great day of unleavened bread he suffered, and they describe Matthew as speaking as they have understood—wherefore their understanding is not in agreement with the law, and according to them the gospels seem to disagree." (*Chron. pasch., praef.*)

3. "The fourteenth is the true passover of the Lord, the great sacrifice, the Son of God in place of the lamb, the bound one who bound the strong, and the judged one, judge of

living and dead; and the one who was given over to the hands of sinners to be crucified, the one who was exalted on the wings of the unicorn, who poured out from his side the two things that purify, water and blood; and the one who was buried on the day of the passover, with a stone placed on the tomb." (*Chron. pasch., praef.*)

XV.—ASIATIC ELDERS IN IRENAEUS

It is doubtful whether more than one elder is being quoted here by Irenaeus, who sometimes refers to the teaching of the elders and of Papias and then quotes Papias (fragment 5 of Papias). Apparently Irenaeus attended lectures by one of them; these are summarized in *Adv. Haer.* iv. 27 *ff.* These elders lived about the middle of the second century, or a little later, as we see from the Ode against Marcus composed by one of them.

1. "Though the precious stone smaragdum is greatly prized by some, yet glass when skilfully made like it puts it to shame, so long as no one is present who can test it and prove that it was made artificially; and when copper is mixed with silver, who can easily test whether it is pure?" (Irenaeus, *Adv. Haer.* i., *praef.*)

2. "Venturesome and bold is the soul warmed by empty air." (*Ibid.* i. 13. 3.)

3. "Idol-maker Marcus, inspector of portents,
   Expert in astrology and the magic art,
   Through which you confirm your false teachings,
   Showing signs to those whom you deceive,
   The works of apostate power,
   Which your father Satan always provides for you
   To work by the power of the angel Azazel;
   He has you as a forerunner of godless wickedness."

   (*Ibid.* i. 15. 6.)

4. "Gypsum mixes badly with the milk of God." (*Ibid*. iii. 17. 4.)

5. "God transferred the curse [of Adam] against the earth, lest it continue against man." (*Ibid*. iii. 23. 3.)

6. "The measureless Father is himself measured in the Son; the Son is the measure of the Father, for he contains him." (*Ibid*. iv. 4. 1.)

7. "Correction provided by the scriptures was enough for the ancients in those matters which they performed without the counsel of the Spirit." (*Ibid*. iv. 27. 1.)

8. "The scripture accused him [Solomon] sufficiently, so that all flesh should not glory in the Lord's sight." (*Ibid*.)

9. "Therefore we should not be proud nor upbraid the ancients, but rather ourselves fear lest, after the recognition of Christ, we should do something displeasing to God, and, no longer having remission of sins, be excluded from his kingdom." (*Ibid*. iv. 27. 2.)

10. "Ignoring the vindications of God and his plans, they, opponents of the Old Testament, condemn themselves." (*Ibid*. iv. 30. 3.)

11. "In regard to the sins for which the scriptures themselves blame the patriarchs and prophets, we should not reprove them nor become like Ham who laughed at his father's shame and fell into wickedness; but rather give thanks to God for them, since at the coming of our Lord their sins were remitted; for he said they gave thanks and rejoiced in our salvation [John viii. 56]. Those whom the scriptures do not blame, but who are simply described, we should not accuse, for we are not more diligent than God, nor can we be above our master, but we ought to seek the type. For nothing is without meaning in those things which are described in the scriptures even without moralizing." (*Ibid*. iv. 31. 1.)

12. "Those who were translated were translated thither

[to Paradise]; for Paradise was prepared for righteous and inspired men. When the apostle was transported into it he heard words which cannot be spoken [2 Cor. xii. 4] to us now; and there the translated ones remain until the end, prepared in advance for incorruption." (Iren., *Adv. Haer.* v. 5, 1).

13. "Through the divine stretching forth of his hands he led the two peoples to one God. For there are two hands because the two peoples are dispersed to the ends of the earth; but one head, for God is one, who is over all and through all and in us all [Eph. iv. 6]." (*Ibid.* v. 17, 4.)

14. "The Son is understood in two ways: first according to nature—he was born a son; second according to what he became—he was considered a son [Rom. i. 3-4]." (*Ibid.* iv. 41, 1.)

15. "Faith occasions this [true comprehension] for us." (Iren., *Epideixis* 3, p. 72, Robinson.)

16. "Now as to the union and concord and peace of the animals of different kinds, which by nature are opposed and hostile to one another, so it will be in truth at the coming of Christ, when he is to reign over all." (*Ibid.* 61, p. 124, Robinson.)

XVI.—POLYCRATES, BISHOP OF EPHESUS

Polycrates, bishop of Ephesus at the end of the second century, was a strong Quartodeciman and defended his party's position against Victor of Rome. He lists his seven relatives who were bishops and celebrated the Passion of the Lord on the fourteenth day of Nisan.

"As for us, then, we keep the day without tampering with it, neither adding nor subtracting. For indeed in Asia great luminaries have fallen asleep, such as shall rise again

6

on the day of the Lord's appearing, when he comes with glory from heaven to seek out all his saints: Philip, one of the twelve apostles, who has fallen asleep in Hierapolis, [as have] also his two daughters who grew old in virginity and his other daughter who lived in the Holy Spirit and rests at Ephesus; and moreover John too, he who 'leant back' on the Lord's 'breast' [John xiii. 25], who was a priest, wearing the sacerdotal plate, both martyr and teacher. He has fallen asleep at Ephesus. Moreover, Polycarp too at Smyrna, both bishop and martyr; and Thraseas, both bishop and martyr, of Eumenia, who has fallen asleep at Smyrna. And why need I mention Sagaris, bishop and martyr, who has fallen asleep at Laodicea? or the blessed Papirius, or Melito the eunuch who in all things lived in the Holy Spirit, who lies at Sardis, awaiting the visitation from heaven, when he shall rise from the dead? These all observed the fourteenth day for the Pascha according to the Gospel, in no way deviating therefrom, but following the rule of faith. And moreover I also, Polycrates, the least of you all, [do] according to the tradition of my relatives, some of whom also I have followed closely. Seven of my relatives were bishops, and I am the eighth. And my relatives always kept the day when the people put away the leaven. Therefore I for my part, brethren, who number sixty-five years in the Lord and have conversed with the brethren from all parts of the world and traversed the entire range of holy Scripture, am not frightened by threats. For those better than I have said, ' We must obey God rather than men' [Acts v. 29]. . . . But I could mention the bishops present with me, whom I summoned when you yourselves desired that I should summon them. And were I to write their names, the number thereof would be great. But they who know my littleness approved my letter, knowing that I did not wear my grey hairs in vain, but that I have ever lived in Christ Jesus." (*H.E.* v. 24. 2-8.)

MARCIONITES AND ANTI-MARCIONITES

XVII.—MARCION

Marcion was not so much an author as an editor (he rewrote either our gospel of Luke or an earlier form of it), and of his original works very little remains. According to Tertullian (*Adv. Marc.* i. 1, iv. 4), he wrote a letter early in his career which showed that his belief was then that of the Church; but this letter has not come down to us. His most prominent work, the *Antitheses*, began thus: "O wealth of riches! Folly, power and ecstasy!—seeing that there can be nothing to say about it, or to imagine about it, or to compare it to!" This sounds much like Karl Barth's position just after the first war, and indeed both men did much to re-emphasize an aspect of Christianity which was in danger of being forgotten. Marcion went on to criticize the Jerusalem apostles as "false brethren," relying on Galatians i-ii; he firmly rejected allegorization of the Old Testament (compare Apelles [XVIII] below). The four chief points of his teaching were derived from New Testament texts. (*a*) No man can serve two masters (Luke xvi. 13)—*i.e.*, the God of the Old Testament and God the Father. (*b*) No man puts a patch of new cloth on an old garment (Luke v. 36)—"Neither Christ nor the apostle is a patch for the Law." (*c*) The Beatitudes. (*d*) "No one is good except the one God, the Father" (Luke xviii. 19).

Harnack's *Marcion* (1924) sets forth all the texts, with a very thorough discussion; see also John Knox, *Marcion and the New Testament* (1942).

(XVIII AND XIX)

Apelles, a disciple of Marcion, was much influenced by Aristotelian logic, and like the followers of Artemon at Rome took delight, not in reading scripture, but in constructing syllogisms based on the literal interpretation of it. His analysis of its contradictions, like the criticism of the literalists whom Philo condemns, seemed blasphemous to allegorizing believers. The *Syllogisms* must have been very long, for Ambrose gives quotations from the 38th book. The last fragment (12) has been handed down among the writings of Irenaeus; but such an ascription is obviously wrong (see Pseudo-Tertullian, 19).

Apelles' opponent Rhodo is known only from his attack against Apelles and from the other brief fragments from Eusebius.

XVIII.—APELLES

Syllogisms

1. "Certain persons raise objections, and especially Apelles, who was the disciple of Marcion but established another heresy greater than the one he took from his master. Now when he wanted to prove that the writings of Moses contain no divine wisdom and none of the work of the Holy Spirit, he exaggerates the things said of this kind and says that in no way could it have been accomplished that in so short a time so many kinds of animals and their foods, which were to last for a whole year, should be taken aboard. For when two by two the impure animals, *i.e.*, two male and two female of each—this is what the repeated word means—and seven by seven the pure animals, that is seven pairs, are described as led into the ark, how, he says, could that space which is described be made big enough to take even four elephants alone? And afterwards he contradicts single points, and on everything adds these words: It is clear that the story is false; but if this be so, it is clear that this scripture is not from God." (Origen, *Hom. in Gen.* ii. 2.)

2. Apelles in the 38th book: "How does the tree of life seem to effect more for life than the breath of God? . . . If God did not make man perfect, but each one through his own industry attains perfection of virtue for himself, does

not man seem to acquire more for himself than God gave him? . . . And if man had not tasted death, he did not know what he had not tasted. Therefore if he had not tasted, he was ignorant; if he was ignorant, he could not fear. Therefore vainly God presented death as a terror, since men did not fear it." (Ambrose, *De Paradiso* v. 28.)

3. "It is not always evil to disobey a precept. For if the precept is good, the obedience is honourable; but if the precept is wicked, it is proper to disobey. Therefore it is not always evil to disobey a good precept. Yet the tree of the knowledge of good and evil is a good work of the Demiurge, since God knew good and evil. . . . Behold Adam was made like one of us. If therefore it is good to have the knowledge of good and evil—and the knowledge which God has is good —he who refuses it to men does not seem to refuse rightly." (*Ibid*. vi. 30.)

4. "He who does not know good and evil is no different from a child; and before a just judge a child is not guilty. A just Demiurge would never have accused a child of crime because of his not knowing good and evil, for a child has no guilt for transgression and crime." (*Ibid*. vi. 31.)

5. "He who does not know good and evil does not even know himself to be evil in not keeping the commandment, nor does he know it to be good to obey evil. And therefore, because he does not know, he who did not obey was worthy of pardon, not condemnation." (*Ibid*. vi. 32.)

6. "Whence did death come to Adam—from the nature of a tree of this sort or indeed from God? If we ascribe it to the nature of the tree, the fruit of this tree seems to excel the life-giving breath of God, if indeed the person whom the breath made alive was brought to death by the fruit of this tree. Or if we say that God is the agent of death we accuse him with a double charge: either he is so harsh that he would not forgive

when he could, or if he could not forgive, so weak." (*Ibid.* vii. 35.)

7. "Did God know Adam would transgress his commandments or did he not? If he did not know, there is no declaration of the divine power; if however he knew and nevertheless gave orders which had to be neglected, it is not godlike to give a superfluous command; yet he gave a superfluous command to that first-formed Adam, which he knew he would not keep at all; yet God does nothing superfluous; therefore the writing is not of God." (*Ibid.* viii. 38.)

8. "Did he know man would sin, he who created him and engraved on him these beliefs about good and evil—or did he not? . . . For there is no human creature made by God which was not commanded by God. Therefore the creation of man is not of God, because God does not make evil; but man accepted the belief about evil when he was told to keep away from evil." (*Ibid.* viii. 40.)

9. "How is God good, when he not only suffered evil to come into this world, but also allowed it to come into such confusion?" (*Ibid.* viii. 41.)

10. "Not only the Jew, but also the heretics who do not accept the Law and the prophets disparage Moses; they even accuse him of crime, saying that Moses was a murderer, for he killed an Egyptian; and with blasphemous tongue they utter many other things against him or against the prophets.'' (Origen, *Hom. in Num.* vii. 1.)

11. "It did not happen thus [as Marcion described it], but Marcion was mistaken. The result was that in all respects his unreason and lawlessness, condemning itself, seemed to turn back against itself, and to raise its own refutation against itself, while the truth remained always firm, needing no aid, but self-sustaining and standing with God who exists for ever. . . . There is one good God, and a single first principle, and a single nameless power; to the one God and

the single principle there is no concern for the things which happen here in this world. But that same holy and good God made from above another god, and the other god created everything, heaven and earth and everything in the world. But he was not all good, and the things made by him were not well made; but everything was created by him according to his evil intelligence." (Epiphanius, *Haer*. xliv. 1.)

12. "How can the serpent, naturally irrational and created mute by God, speak reasonably and vocally? For if of itself it had the ability to reason and judge and understand and reply to the words spoken by the woman, nothing would keep any serpent from doing this. But if they say it addressed Eve with a human voice according to God's will and dispensation, they make God the cause of sin. It was impossible for the evil demon to grant a voice to one naturally mute so that it could be what it was not before; otherwise he would not have stopped conversing with men and leading them astray through serpents and wild animals and birds. And how did an animal hear the commandment which was given secretly by God only to man, without even the woman learning of it? Why did he not attack the man rather than the woman? And if you say that he assaulted the weaker one—on the contrary, she was the stronger, the helper of man, as she was shown in the transgression of the commandment. For she alone resists the serpent, and only after she was beaten by revolt and craft did she eat of the tree. But Adam did not wholly struggle or reply, but took the fruit given by the woman; which is a demonstration of the greatest weakness and an unmanly mind. The woman, overcome by the demon, is worthy of pardon; but Adam, as one overcome by a woman, is not; he himself had received the commandment from God. But the woman, hearing the commandment from Adam, despised it, or thought it unworthy of God to speak it, or doubted it, thinking that Adam had taken it on himself

to give the commandment to her. When she was by herself the serpent found her, so that it could speak privately to her. Seeing her eating the fruits of trees it mentioned the fruit of the tree of knowledge, which was not eaten. And if eaten, obviously it would have been in a corruptible body: For whatever goes into the mouth passes into the drain [Matt. xv. 17]. So if corruptible, then evidently also mortal. And if mortal, no longer a curse, nor was that word spoken to man by the voice of God: Earth thou art, and to earth thou shalt return [Gen. iii. 19]—at least according to the truth of the matters. Again if the serpent did not see the woman eating, how did it induce her to eat when she had never eaten before? And who showed this murderous and criminal serpent that the word of God would have no way out, the word about death which said, 'The day when ye eat, ye shall surely die' [Gen. ii. 17]? Not that alone, but that with this perception their eyes were opened, which did not see before? By this so-called opening they made the approach to death." (Irenaeus, *Frag. Gr.* xiv.)

XIX.—RHODO

At that time also, Rhodo, an Asian by race, a disciple, as he himself records, at Rome of Tatian . . . composed various books, and thus ranged himself along with the rest in opposition to the heresy of Marcion. He records the fact that in his day this heresy was divided up into various opinions; he describes for us who they were who caused the division, and carefully refutes the falsehoods devised by each of them. (*H.E.* v. 13. 1.)

1. "Therefore disagreement has broken out even among themselves, since they contend for an inconsistent opinion. For one of their herd, Apelles, he who plumes himself on his mode of life and old age, acknowledges a single principle, but says that the prophecies come from an enemy spirit—

putting his trust in the utterances of a maiden possessed of a devil, named Philumene. But others, like the sailor Marcion himself, introduce two principles; of these are Potitus and Basilicus. These last, having followed the wolf of Pontus, and failing, as he did, to find the division of things, became reckless, and without any proof baldly asserted two principles. While others, again, of their number, drifting into a worse error, assume not only two, but even three natures. Their leader and chief is Syneros, according to those who shelter themselves behind his school." (*H.E.* v. 13. 2-4.)

2. "For the old man Apelles, when he talked with us, was refuted in many wrong statements. Therefore he went on to allege that one ought not to examine doctrine at all, but that everyone should remain in his own belief. For he asserted that they who place their hopes on the Crucified will be saved, if only they be found in good works. But he held that the most obscure thing of all was, as I have said, the question of God. For he spoke of a single principle, as also our doctrine does." (*H.E.* v. 13. 5.)

3. "But when I said to him, 'Whence do you get this proof? or how can you say that there is a single principle? tell us,' he replied that the prophecies refute themselves, being absolutely devoid of truth; for they are inconsistent and lying and self-contradictory. But as to how there is a single principle, he said he did not know, but that it was merely his impression. Then, on my adjuring him to tell what was true, he swore that he was speaking the truth when he said that he did not understand how there was one un-created God, but that this was his belief. For my part I laughed, and reproved him, because he said he was a teacher, and yet was unable to establish what he taught." (*H.E.* v. 13. 6 *f.*)

4. Now in the same treatise, in addressing Callistio the same writer acknowledges that he had been a disciple of

Tatian at Rome. And he says too that a book of Problems was composed by Tatian. And as its author undertook to present therein the obscure and hidden parts of the divine Scriptures, Rhodo himself promises to give the solutions of Tatian's problems in a special treatise. And there is also extant a memoir of his on the Hexaemeron. (*H.E.* v. 13. 8.)

XX.—MARCIONITE PROLOGUES TO EPISTLES OF PAUL*

About the middle of the second century the Marcionites who were publishing their *Apostolicon* (collection of Paul's letters) felt the need of prologues to emphasize the Marcionite elements in the writings. Great stress is laid on "false apostles," as opposed to *the* apostle of Marcion, Paul.

To the Galatians

Galatians are Greeks. These accepted the word of truth first from the apostle, but after his departure were tempted by false apostles to turn to the law and circumcision. These the apostle recalls to the faith of the truth, writing to them from Ephesus.

To the Corinthians

Corinthians are of Achaia. And these similarly heard the word of truth from the apostle and were perverted variously by false apostles, some by the wordy eloquence of philosophy, others brought in by the sect of the Jewish law. These the apostle recalls to true evangelical wisdom, writing to them from Ephesus by Timothy.

* These are translated by F. C. Burkitt, *The Gospel History and its Transmission*, 355 *f.* The text is given by J. Knox, *Marcion and the New Testament*, 169*f.*

To the Romans

Romans are in the parts of Italy. These were reached beforehand by false apostles, and under the name of our Lord Jesus Christ had been brought in to the law and the prophets. These the apostle recalls to the true evangelical faith, writing to them from Corinth.

To the Thessalonians

Thessalonians are Macedonians, who having accepted the word of truth persevered in the faith even in persecution from their fellow-citizens. Moreover, also, they received not the things said by false apostles. These the apostle praises, writing to them from Athens.

To the Laodiceans

Missing.

To the Colossians

Colossians—these also like the Laodiceans are of Asia, and they had been reached beforehand by pseudo-apostles, nor did the apostle himself come to them. But these also by an epistle he corrects, for they had heard the word from Archippus, who also accepted a ministry unto them. Therefore the apostle already in custody writes to them from Ephesus.

To the Philippians

Philippians are Macedonians. These having accepted the word of truth persevered in the faith, nor did they receive false apostles. These the apostle praises, writing to them from Rome out of prison by Epaphroditus.

To Philemon

To Philemon he sends a private letter for Onesimus his slave, and writes to him from Rome out of prison.

XXI.—ANTI-MARCIONITE PROLOGUES*

Some time between 150 and 180, when the Church in Asia Minor was publishing its set of four canonical gospels in opposition to Marcion's mutilated Luke, these prologues were composed, probably based largely on the work of Papias. The prologue to Matthew and part of that to Mark have been lost; the prologue to John has been tampered with and garbled. The second half of this prologue is apparently based on some phrases in Tertullian.

Mark

. . . Mark related, who was called "Stumpfinger" because for the size of the rest of his body he had fingers that were too short. He was the interpreter of Peter. After Peter's death the same man wrote this gospel in the regions of Italy.

Luke

Luke was a Syrian of Antioch, a physician by profession, a disciple of the apostles and later a follower of Paul until his martyrdom, serving the Lord without distraction, without a wife, without children. At the age of eighty-four he died in Boeotia, full of the Holy Spirit. Although gospels already existed—the one according to Matthew written in Judaea, the one according to Mark in Italy—he was impelled by the Holy Spirit to write this whole gospel among those dwelling about Achaea, making clear in his preface the fact that other gospels were written before his, and that it was necessary to set forth the accurate narrative of the Dispensation to Gentile believers, so that they should not be distracted by Jewish fables nor, deceived by heretical and empty fancies, miss the mark of the truth. As most necessary, then, since it was in the very beginning, we received the birth of John, who is the beginning of the gospel, being the forerunner of the Lord and

* See my article in *Anglican Theological Review*, 23 (1941), 231 *ff*.

sharer in the perfecting of the people and in the institution of baptism and in the fellowship of the passion. Of this dispensation the prophet, one of the twelve [minor prophets], makes mention. And afterward the same Luke wrote the Acts of the Apostles; later John the apostle, one of the Twelve, wrote the Apocalypse on the island of Patmos, and after that the gospel.

John

The gospel of John was revealed and given to the churches by John while he was still in the body, as Papias of Hierapolis, the dear disciple of John, related in the exoteric—that is, in the last—five books, and indeed he wrote down the gospel while John dictated accurately. But the heretic Marcion, since he had been condemned by him because he was opposed to his views, was expelled by John. But in fact he had brought writings or letters to him from the brethren who were in Pontus.

MONTANISTS AND ANTI-MONTANISTS

(XXII—XXIII—XXIV—XXV)

Montanus and his two female attendants, Maximilla and Prisca, were enthusiastic revivalists of the mid-second century. They believed that in Montanus the Paraclete dwelt bodily, and that the heavenly Jerusalem would soon come down at Pepuza in Asia Minor. Their theology is thus largely based on the Johannine writings, which at this time were becoming very popular in Asia, and Gaius of Rome (XXVI) tried to cut the ground from under them by ascribing Gospel and Apocalypse to Cerinthus (Pseudo-Tertullian, 10). The visions and the prophecy of Montanism (which was sometimes called the New Prophecy, XXIII. 1) have been thought of as a return to first-century Christianity; but there is little evidence that, except at Corinth, apostolic Christianity was ordinarily so effervescent.

The anonymous writer composed his treatise against the Montanists thirteen years after Maximilla's death, which probably took place under Marcus Aurelius. It was therefore written in the last decade of the century. His book is dedicated to Avircius Marcellus, whose group of believers may well have been weaker than the Montanists at Hieropolis.

Avircius Marcellus (XXIV) is known to us only from his legendary martyr-acts and from this inscription, which Sir William Ramsay discovered in Phrygia. It has been thought pagan; but it is more likely to come from a persecuted and secretive Christianity. Paul, Faith, the Fish (Ichthys—a symbol of Christ), born of a Virgin, the Eucharistic elements —these are all surely Christian.

Apollonius of Ephesus (XXV) wrote early in the third century, but because of his discussion of Montanus his fragments are included here.

XXII.—MONTANIST ORACLES*

1. Montanus: "I am the Lord God Omnipotent dwelling in man." (Epiphanius, *Haer.* xlviii. 11.)

2. Montanus: "I am neither an angel nor an envoy, but I the Lord God, the Father, have come." (*Ibid.*)

3. Montanus: "I am the Father and the Son and the Paraclete." (Didymus, *De trinitate* iii. 41. 1.)

4. Montanus: "Why do you say 'the superman who is saved'? Because the righteous man will shine a hundred times brighter than the sun, and even the little ones among you who are saved, a hundred times brighter than the moon." (Epiphanius, *Haer.* xlviii. 10.)

5. Montanus: "Behold, man is as a lyre, and I hover over him as a plectrum; man sleeps but I watch; behold, the Lord is removing the hearts of men and giving them (new) hearts." (*Ibid.*, xlviii. 4.)

6. Montanus: "You are exposed to public reproach? It is for your good. He who is not reproached by men is reproached by God. Do not be disconcerted; your righteousness has brought you into the midst (of all). Why are you disconcerted, since you are gaining praise? Your power arises when you are seen by men." (Tertullian, *De fuga* 9.)

7. Montanus: "Do not hope to die in bed nor in abortion nor in languishing fevers, but in martyrdom, that he who suffered for you may be glorified." (*Ibid.*)

8. Montanus: "For God brought forth the Word as a root brings forth a tree, and a spring a river, and the sun a ray." (Tertullian, *Adv. Prax.* 8.)

9. Montanus: "The Church is able to remit sins; but I will not do so, lest others also sin." (Tertullian, *De pudic.* 21.)

10. Maximilla: "After me there will be no more prophecy, but the End." (Epiphanius, *Haer.* xlviii. 11.)

* Assembled in P. de Labriolle, *La crise montaniste* (1913), 34-105.

11. Maximilla: "I am driven as a wolf from the sheep. I am not a wolf; I am word, spirit, and power." (Eusebius, *H.E.* v. 16. 17.)

12. Maximilla: "Do not listen to me, but listen to Christ." (Epiphanius, *Haer.* xlviii. 12.)

13. Maximilla: "The Lord sent me as a partisan of this task, a revealer of this covenant, an interpreter of this promise, forced, whether I will or not, to learn the knowledge of God." (*Ibid.* xlviii. 13.)

14. Prisca: "For continence brings harmony, and they see visions, and, bowing their heads, they also hear distinct voices, saving and mysterious." (Tertullian, *De exh. cast.* 10.)

15. Prisca: "They are flesh, yet they hate the flesh." (Tertullian, *De res. carn.* 11.)

16. Prisca: "Appearing as a woman clothed in a shining robe, Christ came to me [in sleep]; he put wisdom into me and revealed to me that this place is sacred and that here Jerusalem will come down from heaven." (Epiphanius, *Haer.* xlix. 1.)

XXIII.—ANONYMOUS AGAINST MONTANISM

(*H.E.* v. 16 *f.*)

1. "It is a long and very considerable time, beloved Avircius Marcellus, since you urged me to write some kind of treatise against the heresy of the followers of Miltiades, as they are called. Yet I have somehow held back until now, not through lack of ability to refute falsehood and bear witness to the truth, but from fear and extreme caution, lest by chance I might seem to some to be adding a new article or clause to the word of the New Covenant of the gospel, to which no one who has purposed to live according to the

gospel itself may add, and from which no one may take away. But when recently I came to Ancyra in Galatia, and found the local church ringing with the noise of this new (not, as they themselves say, prophecy; but much rather, as will be shown) false prophecy, with the help of the Lord we discoursed, to the best of our ability, for many days in the church on every one of these same points, as well as on those which they put forward. The result was that the church rejoiced greatly and was confirmed in the truth, while they of the contrary side were for the moment discomfited, and the opposers put to grief. So when the local presbyters requested us to leave behind some memorandum of what had been said against them that oppose themselves to the word of truth (and there was present also our fellow-presbyter Zoticus of Otrous), though we did not do this, we promised to write it here, should the Lord permit us, and send it to them speedily."

2. "Their opposition, then, and their recent schismatical heresy as regards the Church, arose thus. There is reported to be a certain village in that Mysia which borders on Phrygia, called by the name of Ardabau. There it is said that a certain recent convert to the faith named Montanus (while Gratus was proconsul of Asia), in the immeasurable longing of his soul for the pre-eminence, first gave the adversary a passage into his heart; and that moved by the spirit he suddenly fell into a state of possession, as it were, and abnormal ecstasy, to such an extent that he became frenzied and began to babble and utter strange sounds, that is to say, prophesying contrary to the manner which the Church had received from generation to generation by tradition from the beginning. Some of those who heard at that time his spurious utterances were annoyed at him, as at one possessed and tormented by a demon, the prey of a spirit of error and a disturber of the people. So they rebuked and strove to check his speaking, mindful of the injunction and warning of the

7

Lord to guard watchfully against the coming of false prophets [Matt. vii. 15]. But others were puffed up, as if at a
prophetical gift of the Holy Spirit, and filled with no slight
conceit, and forgetful of the Lord's injunction. Therefore
they called forth this maddening and cajoling spirit which
was deceiving the people, by which they were beguiled and
deceived, so that it could no longer be checked to silence.
And by some art, or rather by the employment of such an
evil artifice, the devil secretly stirred up and inflamed the
minds which had lost in sleep the true faith, those of the
disobedient persons whose ruin he had devised, and by whom
—accordingly!—he was honoured. So that he raised up two
women as well, and so filled them with the spurious spirit
that they too babbled in a frenzied, inopportune and un-
natural manner, like him whom we mentioned above. And
the spirit pronounced them blessed who rejoiced and prided
themselves in him, and puffed them up with the greatness of
his promises; yet at times he would administer shrewd and
plausible rebukes to their face, that he might seem capable of
reproving also. Nevertheless, there were few who were thus
deceived by the Phrygians. Moreover, this arrogant spirit
taught them to blaspheme the entire universal Church under
heaven, because the spirit of false prophecy received neither
honour nor admission into it. For when the faithful throughout Asia had met frequently and at many places in Asia for
this purpose, and on examination of the new-fangled
teachings had pronounced them profane, and rejected the
heresy, these persons were thus expelled from the Church
and shut off from its fellowship."

3. "Since, then, they also used to call us slayers of the
prophets [Matt. xxiii. 31] because we did not receive their
prophets of unbridled tongue (for these, they say, are they
whom the Lord promised to send to the people), let them
answer us before God: Is there a single one, gentlemen, of

these followers of Montanus or of the women who began to babble, who was persecuted by Jews or killed by lawless men? None. Or were any of them seized and crucified for the Name's sake? No. Or, indeed, were any of the women ever scourged in the synagogues of the Jews or stoned? Never in any way. No, it was another death that Montanus and Maximilla are reported to have died. For report says that a maddening spirit drove both of them to hang themselves, though not at the same time; and a persistent rumour at the time of each death said that thus they died and ended their life, after the fashion of the traitor Judas. Similarly, common report has it about that marvellous man, the—so to speak—first steward of their so-called prophecy, Theodotus, that once, on being lifted and raised heavenwards, he fell into abnormal ecstasy, and entrusting himself to the spirit of error was whirled to the ground, and so met a miserable end. But, my dear sir, let us not imagine we can be certain of a fact of this kind when we did not see it. Perhaps it was thus, perhaps it was not thus, that Montanus and Theodotus and the previously mentioned woman met their end."

4. "And let not the spirit which spoke in the person of Maximilla say in the same book *According to Asterius Urbanus*, 'I am driven as a wolf from the sheep. I am not a wolf. I am word and spirit and power' [Montanist Oracles, 11]. But let him show clearly the power that is in the spirit, let him bring convincing proof of it, and by the spirit let him force an acknowledgement from those who were then present to prove and discourse with the talkative spirit. Approved men and bishops, Zoticus from the village of Cumana and Julian from Apamea, whose mouths the followers of Themiso muzzled, and would not allow them to refute the false spirit which was deceiving the people."

5. "And surely this falsehood too is now evident. For it is more than thirteen years today since the woman died, and

there has been neither a partial nor a universal war in the world. Instead, by God's mercy the Christians have enjoyed continuous peace."

6. "So then when refuted in all their arguments they are at a loss, they endeavour to take refuge in the martyrs, saying that they have many martyrs, and that this is a reliable proof of the power of that which is called among them the prophetic spirit. But this, as it appears, proves to be absolutely untrue. For it is a fact that some of the other heresies have immense numbers of martyrs, yet surely we shall not for this reason give them our assent, nor acknowledge that they possess the truth. To take them first, those called Marcionites from the heresy of Marcion say that they have immense numbers of martyrs of Christ, but as regards Christ himself they do not truly acknowledge him."

7. "It is doubtless for this reason that whenever those called from the Church to martyrdom for the true faith meet with any so-called martyrs from the heresy of the Phrygians, they separate themselves from them and are perfected without having fellowship with them, for they do not wish to assent to the spirit which spoke through Montanus and the women. And that this is true, and that it took place in our time at Apamea on the Meander among those martyrs of Eumenia who were the companions of Gaius and Alexander, is an evident fact."

8. "I found these things in a certain treatise of theirs, in which they attack that treatise of our brother Miltiades in which he shows that a prophet ought not to speak in a state of ecstasy; and I abridged them."

9. " . . . but the false prophet in abnormal ecstasy, upon whom follow licence and fearlessness. For while he begins with voluntary ignorance, he ends with involuntary madness of soul, as has been stated. But they cannot show any prophet under either the Old or the New [Prophecy] who was moved

by the Spirit after this manner, neither Agabus nor Judas nor Silas nor the daughters of Philip, nor Ammia in Philadelphia nor Quadratus, nor can they make their boast of any others whatever not belonging to their number."

10. "For if, as they say, the women followers of Montanus succeeded to the prophetic gift after Quadratus and Ammia of Philadelphia, let them show which of their number, who were followers of Montanus and the women, succeeded to it. For the Apostle lays it down that the prophetic gift ought to continue in the whole Church until the Lord's coming. But they cannot produce anyone, though it is the fourteenth year or thereabouts since the death of Maximilla."

XXIV.—AVIRCIUS MARCELLUS, BISHOP (?) OF HIEROPOLIS

1. (An anti-Montanist writer says) "As for a long and very great time, beloved Avircius Marcellus, I have been urged by you to compose some writings against the heresy called after Miltiades. . . ." (*H.E.* v. 16. 3.)

2. "I a citizen of the elect city erected this
in my lifetime, that I might have before me a place for
my body;
my name is Avircius, a disciple of the pure Shepherd
who feeds the flocks of sheep on mountains and
plains,

5 who has great all-seeing eyes;
he taught me . . . faithful scriptures.
To Rome he sent me to see my king
and to see the queen, golden-robed and golden
sandalled;
a people I saw there which has a splendid seal,

10 and I saw the plain and all the towns of Syria, and
Nisibis,

crossing the Euphrates; but everywhere I met with
fellows;
Paul was my companion, and Faith everywhere led the
way
and served food everywhere, the Fish from the spring
—immense, pure, which the pure Virgin caught
15 and gave to her friends to eat for ever,
with good wine, giving the cup with the loaf.
These things I Avircius said to be written thus in my
presence.
I am truly seventy-two years old.
Let everyone who knows these things, and is in agreement, pray for Avircius.
20 No one is to put anyone else into my tomb;
otherwise he is to pay the Roman treasury 2,000 gold
pieces
and (my) good native city of Hieropolis 1,000 gold
pieces."

(W. M. Ramsay, *Cities and Bishoprics of Phrygia*, ii. 657.)

XXV.—APOLLONIUS OF EPHESUS

(*H.E.* v. 18.)

1. "But his works and teaching show of what kind this
new-fangled teacher [Montanus] is. This is he who taught
dissolutions of marriages; who laid down laws on fasting;
who named Pepuza and Tymion [small towns in Phrygia]
Jerusalem, in his desire to draw to them people from everywhere; who appointed agents for collecting money; who has
devised his scheme for receiving gifts, under the name of
'offerings'; who has supplied salaries to those who preach his
doctrine, so that by means of gluttony the teaching of it may
be more effective."

2. "We show, therefore, that these prophetesses were the very first, from the time when they were filled with the spirit, who left their husbands. How, then, did they speak falsehood, calling Priscilla a virgin?"

3. "Does not every scripture seem to you to forbid a prophet to receive gifts and money [see Didache 11 f.]? Therefore, when I see the prophetess possessed of gold and silver and costly apparel, how can I fail to reject her?"

4. "Moreover, Themiso too, he who is clothed with plausible covetousness, who did not bear the sign of confession, but put off his chains, thanks to a large sum of money, and (though this fact should have made him humble) boasts himself a martyr—this man, imitating the Apostle, dared to compose a 'catholic epistle,' and in it to instruct those whose faith had surpassed his, to contend with empty-sounding words, and to utter blasphemy against the Lord, the apostles and the holy Church."

5. "But not to speak of many, let the prophetess tell us about Alexander, who calls himself a martyr, with whom she banquets, to whom also many do reverence. It is not for us to speak of his robberies, and the other deeds of daring for which he has been punished—the record office preserves the tale of them. Which, then, of the two forgives the other's sins? Does the prophet forgive the martyr his robberies, or the martyr the prophet his deeds of covetousness? For though the Lord has said, 'Get you no gold, nor silver, nor two coats' [Matt. x. 9 f.], they, in complete contradiction, have transgressed as regards the getting of these forbidden things. For we shall show that they whom they call prophets and martyrs get their petty gains not only from the rich but also from poor people and orphans and widows. And if they are confident, let them take their stand on this, and come to a definite agreement on this understanding, that if convicted they may at least for the future cease to transgress. For one

ought to prove the fruits of the prophet: for the tree is known by its fruit. But, that those who wish may know about Alexander, he has been convicted by Aemilius Frontinus, proconsul at Ephesus, not because of the Name, but because of the robberies he committed, being already an apostate. Next, he made a false appeal to the Name of the Lord and was released, having deceived the faithful in that city. And his own community, whence he came, would not receive him, because he was a robber. Those who desire to learn about him have the public archives of Asia. And yet the prophet knows nothing of him with whom he associated many years! In exposing this man we also expose, by means of him, his claim to be a prophet. We can show the same in the case of many; and if they have the courage, let them stand the exposure!"

6. "If they deny that their prophets have received gifts, let them agree on this point, that if they are convicted of having received them, they are not prophets; and we will furnish countless demonstrations of the fact. But one must prove all the fruits of a prophet. Tell me, does a prophet dye his hair? Does a prophet paint his eyelids? Does a prophet love adornment? Does a prophet play at gaming tables and dice? Does a prophet lend money at interest? Let them agree whether these things are permitted or not, and for my part I will show that they took place among them."

XXVI.—GAIUS OF ROME

Gaius, a "very learned" Roman presbyter, was so vehemently anti-Montanist that he rejected the Gospel and Apocalypse of John, ascribing them to Cerinthus. Like the Alogi whom Epiphanius describes, he compared the Fourth Gospel with the Synoptics and found the Apocalypse in disagreement with the eschatology of authentic scripture.

Dialogue with Proclus

1. "But I can point out the trophies of the apostles. For if you are willing to go to the Vatican, or to the Ostian Way, you will find the trophies of those who founded the church." (*H.E.* ii. 25. 7.)

2. "But Cerinthus too, by means of revelations supposed to be written by a great apostle, falsely introduces wonderful stories to us as if they had been shown to him by angels. He says that, after the resurrection, Christ's kingdom will be on earth, and the flesh, dwelling at Jerusalem, will again serve lusts and pleasures. And being an enemy to God's scriptures, and wishing to deceive, he says that there will be a period of a thousand years for wedding festivities." (*H.E.* iii. 28. 2.)

3. "Proclus speaks thus: But after him there were at Hierapolis in Asia four prophetesses, daughters of Philip. Their tomb is there, and that of their father." (*H.E.* iii. 31. 4.)

4. While curbing the recklessness and audacity of his opponents in composing new scriptures, he mentions only thirteen epistles of the holy apostle, not numbering the Epistle to the Hebrews with the rest; as there are even to this day some among the Romans who do not consider it to be the apostle's. (*H.E.* vi. 20. 3.)

Dialogue with Proclus* (?)

5. "These things [described in Rev. viii. 7-11] are not what will take place; for the coming of the Lord will take place as a thief by night." (Dionysius Bar Salibi, *In Apoc.*, *Actus et Epist. canon.*, interp. I. Sedlacek, p. 8.)

6. "As in the flood the heavenly bodies were not taken away, so at the End it will happen, according to the scripture [Matt. xxiv. 37] and the writing of Paul—when they say

---

* Fragments from Bar Salibi in P. de Labriolle, *La crise montaniste*.

peace and security, then their destruction will be at hand."
[1 Thess. v. 3; against Rev. viii. 12.] (*Ibid.* p. 9.)

7. "How can the lawless be tormented by locusts [Rev. ix.
3-5] when the scripture says that sinners prosper and the
righteous are persecuted in the world [Ps. lxxiii. 2, Job
xxi. 9?]?, and Paul says that believers shall be persecuted and
evil men shall grow worse, deceiving and deceived [2 Tim.
iii. 12 *f.*]?" (*Ibid.* p. 10.)

8. "It is not written that angels shall war nor that a quarter
of mankind shall be destroyed [Rev. ix. 14 *ff.*], but that nation
shall rise against nation [Matt. xxiv 7]." (*Ibid.* p. 10.)

9. "How can Satan be bound here [Rev. xx. 2] when it is
written that Christ entered into the house of the strong man
and bound him and took away his goods from him [Matt.
xii. 29]?" (*Ibid.* p. 19.)

10. Hippolytus of Rome said: There was a man named
Gaius who claimed that neither the Gospel nor the Apo-
calypse were John's, but rather belonged to the heretic
Cerinthus. (*Ibid.* p. 1.)

11. The heretic Gaius charged John with disagreeing with
his fellow-evangelists since he says that after the baptism he
went into Galilee and wrought the miracle of the wine at
Cana. (P. de Labriolle, *La crise montaniste*, p. 285.)

Fragments of the Alogi

The arguments used against the Johannine writings by
this group are so similar to those of Gaius that it is probable
that either he was a member of their group or else late writers
against heretics have ascribed his writings to them. The
remains of the Alogi are therefore included among the
fragments of Gaius.

12. They say that these books are not by John but by
Cerinthus, and are not worthy to be [read] in church.
(Epiphanius, *Haer.* li. 3.)

13. They say that his books do not agree with the other apostles. "What does he say? 'In the beginning was the Logos, and the Logos was with God, and the Logos was God,' and 'the Logos became flesh and tabernacled among us, and we beheld his glory, glory as of the Only-begotten of the Father, full of grace and truth,' and directly following, 'John bore witness and cried, saying, This is he of whom I spoke to you, and, This is the Lamb of God, who takes away the sin of the world,' and after that it says, 'And they who heard said to him, Rabbi, where do you dwell?' And in the same place, 'The next day Jesus wanted to go to Galilee, and he finds Philip and says to him, Follow me.' And a little beyond this, 'And after three days there was a wedding in Cana of Galilee, and Jesus was invited to the wedding, and his disciples with him, and his mother was there.' But the other evangelists say that he spent forty days in the desert, tempted by the devil, and then returned and took the disciples to himself." (Epiphanius, *Haer*. li. 4.)

14. "Behold, the second gospel [Mark] makes it clear concerning Christ, yet nowhere mentions being born again [John iii. 3]; but it says, 'In the Jordan the Spirit came upon him, and a voice, This is the beloved Son, in whom I am well pleased' [Mark i. 9-11]." (Epiphanius, *Haer*. li. 6.)

15. "The gospel written in the name of John is false. For after saying, 'The Logos became flesh and tabernacled among us,' and a few other things, it immediately says, 'There was a wedding in Cana of Galilee.'" (Epiphanius, *Haer*. li. 18.)

16. They say that since the gospel according to John does not say the things (as the other gospels) it is uncanonical (*adiatheton*), and they will not accept it. (Epiphanius, *Haer*. i. 18.)

17. "John spoke of the Saviour's keeping two passovers, but the other evangelists, only one." (Epiphanius, *Haer*. li. 22.)

18. We also find expressed somewhere in these writings that the divine Logos was begotten of God in the fortieth year of Augustus. Either the writer was mistaken, or through the *beta*'s dropping out and only the *mu* remaining, he wrote only *mu* (forty) years. For he was begotten in the forty-second year of Augustus. He also says that it was on the twelfth day before the calends of July or June, I do not remember which, in the consulship of Sulpicius Camerinus and Vettius Pompeianus. I noticed this because those who mention the day of the conception, when Gabriel told the news to the Virgin, share the opinion of some who say that according to tradition he was born in seven months. (Epiphanius, *Haer.* li. 29.)

19. "Of what value to me is the Apocalypse of John, which tells about seven angels and seven trumpets [Rev. viii. 2]?" (Epiphanius, *Haer.* li. 32.)

20. "Again it says, 'Write to the angel of the church in Thyatira' [Rev. ii. 18]; and there was no church at all there in Thyatira. How then did he write to a non-existent church?" (Epiphanius, *Haer.* li. 33.)

21. These incompetent word-chasers reject the gospel and apocalypse of John, and even his epistles, which agree with the gospel and apocalypse. And they say, " 'I saw, and he said to the angel, Loose the four angels which are in the Euphrates. And I heard the number of the army, ten thousand times ten thousand, and a thousand times a thousand, and they were clad in breastplates of fire and brimstone and hyacinth! [Rev. ix. 14-7].' " They think that the truth is ridiculous. (Epiphanius, *Haer.* li. 34.)

ROMANS AND THEIR FRIENDS

XXVII.—MARTYRDOM OF JUSTIN*

The Martyrdom of Justin (about 160) is interesting not only for its realistic trial reporting, but for the light cast on Christian teaching methods in the capital of the empire. Justin evidently had his own school which met regularly and trained catechumens for the Roman church. Some of them were taught by their parents, but received advanced instruction in the school of Christian philosophy.

In the time of the lawless proponents of idolatry an impious edict against the pious Christians was set forth in every city and region, to force them to sacrifice to vain idols. When they were apprehended the holy men were brought before the prefect of Rome, Rusticus by name. When they had been brought before the tribunal, Rusticus the prefect said to Justin, "First, believe in the gods and obey the emperors." Justin said, "It is not blameworthy or reprehensible to believe in the precepts of our Saviour Jesus Christ." Prefect Rusticus said, "What precepts do you profess?" Justin said, "All the sayings I undertook to learn; I adhere to the true sayings of the Christians, though they do not please those of false opinions." The prefect Rusticus said, "Those sayings please you, you wretch?" Justin said, "Yes, since I follow them with the right dogma." The prefect Rusticus said, "What is that dogma?" Justin said, "That we worship the God of the Christians, whom we think to be one, from the beginning maker and creator of the whole creation, visible and invisible; and the Lord Jesus Christ the Son of God, who was predicted by the prophets as going to

* In R. Knopf-G. Krüger, *Ausgewählte Märtyrerakfen*, 15 *ff*.

come to the human race, herald of salvation and teacher of good precepts. And since I am a mere man, I think I can say little about his boundless Godhead, but I confess that I need some prophetic power; because it was foretold of him whom I mentioned that he was Son of God. For I know that of old the prophets spoke of his coming, which was going to take place among men."

The prefect Rusticus said, "Where do you meet?" Justin said, "Where each one chooses and is able. For do you think we all come together in the same place? Not at all; for the God of Christians is not limited by place, but being invisible fills heaven and earth and everywhere is worshipped and glorified by the faithful." The prefect Rusticus said, "Tell me, where do you meet, or in what place do you gather your disciples?" Justin said, "I live above the bath of a certain Martin, the son of Timothinus, and during all this time (this is my second stay in the city of Rome) I have not known any other assembly but the one there. And whoever wanted to come to me, to him I communicated the words of truth." Rusticus said, "Well, finally, you are a Christian?" Justin said, "Yes, I am a Christian."

The prefect Rusticus said to Chariton, "And tell me, Chariton, are you a Christian too?" Chariton said, "I am a Christian, by God's command." The prefect Rusticus said to Charito, "What do you say, Charito?" Charito said, "I am a Christian, by God's gift." Rusticus said to Euelpistus, "And what are you?" Euelpistus, an imperial slave, replied, "I too am a Christian, freed by Christ, and I share the same hope, thanks to Christ." The prefect Rusticus said to Hierax, "Are you a Christian too?" Hierax said, "Yes, I am a Christian, for I worship and adore the same God." The prefect Rusticus said, "Did Justin make you a Christian?" Hierax replied, "I have been a Christian a long time, and I [always] will be one." Paeon, who was just standing there, said, "I too am a Christian." The prefect Rusticus said, "Who taught you?" Paeon said, "From our parents we received this good confession." Euelpistus said, "I gladly heard Justin's discourses, but I too received my Christian training from my parents." The prefect Rusticus said, "Where are your parents?" Euelpistus said, "In Cappadocia." Rusticus said to Hierax, "Where are *your* parents?" He answered and said, "Our true father is Christ, and our mother is faith in him. My earthly parents are dead, and I came here after being abducted from Phrygian Iconium." The prefect Rusticus said to Liberianus, "And what do you say? Are you a Christian? Aren't you religious [instead]?" Liberianus said, "I too am a Christian; I *am* religious, for I worship the only true God."

The prefect said to Justin, "Listen, you who are called learned and think you know true dogmas; if you are beaten and beheaded, do you believe you are going to go up into the sky?" Justin said, "I hope I will have Christ's rewards if I endure these things. For I know that for all who live thus there is waiting until the end of the world a divine gift of grace." The prefect Rusticus said, "So you suppose you will go up into the sky to receive some compensation?" Justin said, "I do not suppose so, I know so, and am certain of it." The prefect Rusticus said, "Well, suppose we come to the point and do our business. Come together there, and all together sacrifice to the gods!" Justin said, "No right-thinking man falls from religion into irreligion." Rusticus said, "If you do not obey, you will be tortured without mercy." Justin said, "We have this in our prayer—to be saved even in tortures through our Lord Jesus Christ, for this will be our salvation and encouragement before the more terrible tribunal, the universal one of our Lord and Saviour." So spoke the other martyrs too; [they said,] "Do what you will; for we are Christians, and do not sacrifice to idols."

The prefect Rusticus answered and said, "Those who refuse to sacrifice to the gods and to keep the decree of the emperor are to be beaten and taken away to suffer capital punishment, in obedience to the laws."

The holy martyrs, glorifying God, came out to the appointed place and were beheaded, thus perfecting their testimony in the Saviour's confession. Some of the faithful secretly took away their bodies and put them in a suitable place, being helped by the grace of our Lord Jesus Christ, to whom be glory for ever and ever. Amen.

XXVIII.—DIONYSIUS OF CORINTH

Dionysius of Corinth, writing to Rome about 160, shows us a vigorous bishop engaged in attacking heresy, in instructing catechumens, in thanking the Roman church for its gifts and in conducting the liturgy, during which was read Clement's letter to the Corinthians as well as a later one from Soter. The Roman church is increasing its already strong ascendancy, especially in regard to this church of Corinth, which was bound to Rome not only by bonds of the spirit but by ties of trade. Dionysius also condemns the Marcionite custom of excising parts of scripture as not genuine.

And first of all it should be said of Dionysius, that he had been entrusted with the throne of the episcopate of the community at Corinth, and that he used to communicate without stint of his inspired industry, not only with those under his charge but also with those in foreign lands, rendering himself of the greatest service to all in the catholic epistles which he penned to the churches. Of these one is addressed to the Lacedaemonians, containing instruction in orthodoxy and exhorting to peace and unity; another to the Athenians, stirring them up to faith and that conduct which is in accordance with the Gospel, which conduct he convicts of esteeming lightly, in that they had all but apostatized from the Word from the time that it befell their president Publius to suffer martyrdom in the persecution of that day. And he mentions that Quadratus was appointed their bishop after the martyred Publius, and testifies that by his zeal they were brought together again and had their faith rekindled. And moreover he informs us that Dionysius the Areopagite, whom the apostle Paul converted to the faith according to the account in the Acts, had been the first to be entrusted with the episcopate of the community at Athens. And there is extant another epistle of his, to the Nicomedians, in which he attacks the heresy of Marcion and defends the canon of the truth. And in writing also to the church which sojourns in Gortyna together with the other communities in Crete, he commends their bishop Philip, because the church under him had witness borne to it for very many deeds of bravery, and reminds him of the need of guarding against the perversion of the heretics. And in writing also to the church which sojourns in Amastris together with the churches in Pontus, he mentions that Bacchylides and Elpistus had urged him to write; and he has set out expositions of the divine Scriptures, indicating their bishop Palmas by name. And he gives the same people much exhortation on the subjects of marriage and chastity, and orders that those who come back from any falling away whatsoever, whether it be a fault [of conduct] or even a wandering into heresy, should be welcomed. With these has been included another epistle, to the Cnossians, in which he counsels Pinytus, the bishop of the community, not to lay a heavy burden, that of chastity, as a necessary thing, upon the brethren, but to have an eye to the weakness of the many. In his reply to this Pinytus admires and commends Dionysius, but in his turn counsels him to impart on some future occasion more solid food, and nourish his people with a further letter for men more fully grown; so that from continual converse with doctrines of milk they might not

8

grow old imperceptibly under a training fit for babes. And in this epistle also Pinytus' orthodoxy in the faith, his care for the profit of his hearers, his learning and understanding of divine things, are revealed, so to speak, under the most perfect of images. (*H.E.* iv. 23. 1-9.)

Dionysius to the Romans, to Soter, then Bishop

1. "For this has been your custom from the beginning: to do good in divers ways to all the brethren, and to send supplies to many churches in every city, now relieving the poverty of the needy, now making provision, by the supplies which you have been in the habit of sending from the beginning, for brethren in the mines. And thus as Romans you observe the hereditary custom of Romans, which your blessed bishop Soter has not only maintained, but even advanced, by providing in abundance the help that is distributed for the use of the saints, and by exhorting with blessed words, as a loving father his children, the brethren who come up [to Rome]." (*H.E.* iv. 23. 10.)

2. "In these ways you also, by such an admonition, have united the planting that came from Peter and Paul, of both the Romans and the Corinthians. For indeed both planted also in our Corinth, and likewise taught us; and likewise they taught together also in Italy, and were martyred on the same occasion." (*H.E.* ii. 25. 8.)

3. "This day, therefore, we spent as a holy Lord's day, in which we read your epistle; from the reading of which we shall always be able to obtain admonition, as also from the former epistle written to us through Clement." (*H.E.* iv. 23. 11.)

4. "For when the brethren desired me to write epistles, I did so. And these the apostles of the devil have filled with tares, cutting out some things and adding others: for whom the woe is reserved. It is not marvellous, therefore, if some

3. ". . . among whom the elders before Soter, who presided over the church of which you are now the leader—we mean Anicetus and Pius, Hyginus and Telesphorus and Xystus—neither themselves observed it nor permitted those [residing] with them [to do so]; and none the less, though themselves not observing it, they were at peace with the members of the communities where it was observed, when the latter came to them. And yet the observance was the more obnoxious to those who did not observe it. And none were ever expelled because of this course of action, but those very elders before you, though they did not observe it, would send the eucharist to members of those communities who observed it. And when the blessed Polycarp stayed at Rome in the time of Anicetus, though they had some trifling disagreements on other matters, they immediately made peace nor did they care to quarrel on this subject. For neither could Anicetus persuade Polycarp not to observe what he had always observed with John the disciple of the Lord and the other apostles with whom he consorted; nor yet did Polycarp persuade Anicetus to observe it, for he said that he ought to hold to the custom of the elders before him. And though such was the case, they held communion with one another, and in the church Anicetus yielded the [celebration of the] eucharist to Polycarp, obviously out of respect. So they parted from one another in peace and the whole Church was at peace, both they who observed and they who did not." (*H.E.* v. 24. 14-17.)

XXX.—MURATORIAN FRAGMENT

The Muratorian fragment represents the state of the New Testament canon at Rome about 180. The Four Gospels are fixed, though John still needs defence more than the others (compare XXVI). The epistles of Paul do not include Hebrews, and in addition to the Apocalypse of John there is that of Peter, which is not so cordially received. The Petrine epistles are not mentioned, though the writer speaks of the book of Wisdom (in the New Testament?). The Shepherd of Hermas is rejected for public reading since it was composed only recently. Heretical works are resolutely opposed. Only a corrupt Latin version is extant.

". . . at which he was present, and thus he wrote them down. The third book of the gospel is according to Luke. Luke the physician, when Paul had taken him with him after the ascension of Christ, as one skilled in writing, wrote from report in his own name, though he did not himself see the Lord in the flesh; and on that account, as he was able to ascertain events, so he set them down. So he began his story from the birth of John. The Fourth Gospel is of John, one of the disciples. To his fellow-disciples and bishops, who were encouraging him, he said, 'Fast with me today for three days, and whatever will be revealed to each of us, let us tell to one another.' The same night it was revealed to Andrew, one of the apostles, that all should certify what John wrote in his own name. Therefore, while various elements may be taught in the several books of gospels, it makes no difference to the faith of believers, for by the one chief Spirit all things have been declared in all: concerning the nativity, the passion, the resurrection, the life with his disciples, and his double advent, first in lowliness and contempt (which has taken place), second in glorious royal power (which is to be). Why, then, is it remarkable that John so constantly brings forth single points even in his epistles, saying of himself, 'What we have seen with our eyes and heard with our ears and our hands have handled, these we write to you?' Thus he professes himself not only a witness and hearer but also a writer of all the miracles of the Lord in order. The Acts of all the apostles are written in one book. Luke has included for 'good Theophilus' the things which were done in his presence, as the omission of Peter's passion clearly shows, and the departure of Paul from town on his way to Spain. The epistles of Paul themselves make clear, to those who wish to understand, what they are, from what place or why they were sent; the first of all to the Corinthians forbidding schism and heresies: then to the Galatians forbidding circumcision; to the Romans next he wrote more fully, telling them the order of the scriptures and the fact that their first principle is Christ. It is necessary for us to discuss these one by one because the blessed apostle Paul himself, following the order of his predecessor John, writes only by name to seven churches, in this order: to the Corinthians first, to the Ephesians second, to the Philippians third, to the Colossians fourth, to the Galatians fifth, to the Thessalonians sixth, to the Romans seventh. While to the Corinthians and Thessalonians it was repeated for their admonition, yet it is known that one church is diffused throughout the whole world. And while John in the Apocalypse writes to seven churches, yet he speaks to all. But to Philemon one and to Titus one and to Timothy two for affection and love, yet they are sanctified in honour with the Catholic church for ordaining ecclesiastical discipline. There is current one to the Laodiceans, another to the Alexandrians forged in Paul's name for the heresy of Marcion, and several others which cannot be accepted in the Catholic church; for it is not suitable to mix gall with honey. The epistle of Jude and two bearing the name of John are accepted in the Catholic church, and Wisdom, written by the friends of Solomon in his honour. We accept the apocalypses only of John and Peter, which some of us do not allow to be read in churches. But the Shepherd was written very recently, in our own times in the city of Rome, by Hermas when bishop Pius his brother was occupying the chair of the city of Rome; and therefore, while it is proper for it to be read, it cannot be publicly read in church to the people to the end of time, either among the prophets, whose number is complete, or among the apostles. But of Arsinous or Valentinus or Miltiades we accept nothing at all [or] those who wrote a new book of psalms for Marcion, along with Basilides [and] the Asiatic founder of the Cataphrygians. (Routh i. 393 *ff.*; H. Lietzmann, *Kleine Texte* i.)

XXXI.—PASSION OF THE SCILLITAN MARTYRS

To conclude our fragments we give the Scillitan martyrdom, an authentic court record of 180, the year when the man mentioned as consul held office. Tertullian names the proconsul Saturninus as the first to draw the sword on Christians in Africa. How the church of Carthage declined from the firm otherworldly faith of this period may be seen from an investigation before another proconsul in the year 320, when the bishop was accused not only of ordaining for money but of stealing valuables from the temple of Serapis. But here there is no hint of decline; here they reign with the Father and the Son and the Holy Spirit for ever and ever.

In the consulship of Praesens (for the second time) and Claudianus, the 16th before the Calends of August, into the senate house of Carthage were brought Speratus, Nartzalus and Cittinus, Donata, Secunda, Vestia, to whom the proconsul Saturninus said, "You may receive indulgence from our Lord the Emperor if you return to good sense." Speratus said, "We have never done evil, we have done no iniquitous deed, we have never cursed, but when we were received badly we gave thanks; for we serve our ruler." The proconsul Saturninus said, "We too are religious, and our religion is simple—we swear by the genius of our Lord the Emperor, and we pray for his safety, which you should do too." Speratus said, "If you will lend an ear, calmly, I will tell you the mystery of simplicity." Saturninus said, "I will not lend an ear to you, who are about to say evil things about our rites; on the contrary, swear by the genius of our Lord the Emperor." Speratus said, "I do not recognize the authority of this age; rather I serve that God whom no man sees nor can see with these eyes. I have not committed theft, but if I have bought anything I have paid the tax. For I recognize my Lord, the king of kings and ruler of all nations." The proconsul Saturninus said to the rest, "Abandon this persuasion." Speratus said, "It is an evil persuasion to commit murder, to speak false witness." The proconsul Saturninus said, "Do not share in this madness." Cittinus said, "There is no one whom we fear except the Lord our God who is in heaven." Donata said, "Honour to Caesar as Caesar, but fear to God." Vestia said, "I am a Christian." Secunda said, "What I am, I want to remain." The proconsul Saturninus said, "Do you persevere in being a Christian?" Speratus said, "I am a Christian"; and they all agreed with him. The proconsul Saturninus said, "Do you want some time to consider?" Speratus said, "In so just an affair there is no need of considering." The proconsul Saturninus said, "What things do you have in your box?" Speratus said, "The books, and the epistles of Paul, a good man." The proconsul Saturninus said, "Take a stay of thirty days and reconsider." Speratus again said, "I am a Christian"; and they all agreed with him. The proconsul Saturninus read the decree from the tablet: "Speratus, Nartzalus, Cittinus, Donata, Vestia, Secunda, and the others who confessed that they live after the Christian fashion, since after opportunity was offered them of returning to the Roman way they persevered obstinately, let them be punished by the sword." Speratus said, "We give thanks to God." Nartzalus said, "To-day we are martyrs in heaven; thanks be to God." The proconsul Saturninus ordered it spoken by a herald:

"Speratus, Nartzalus, Cittinus, Veturius, Felix, Aquilinus, Laetantius, Januarius, Generosa, Vestia, Donata, Secunda are ordered to be executed." Everyone said, "Thanks be to God." And so they all were crowned with martyrdom at the same time, and they reign with the Father and the Son and the Holy Spirit for ever and ever. Amen. (In R. Knopf-G. Kruger, *Ausgewählte Märtyrerakten*, 28 *f*.)

PSEUDO-TERTULLIAN AGAINST ALL HERESIES

When Hippolytus was bishop in Rome, seventeen centuries ago, he composed a work against all heresies. This was his *Syntagma*, written about 200-210, and in it he included much of the material his teacher Irenaeus had used, as well as personal observations and hearsay. Irenaeus had written against heresies about 180. Since his time had risen Theodotus of Byzantium and Theodotus the money-changer, as well as the modalists Praxeas and Noetus; the Valentinian Heracleon had come into prominence, as had Marcion's followers Lucan and Apelles. Montanism seemed more menacing than Irenaeus had thought. A new edition of his five books, at the very least, was required. This Hippolytus set himself to provide, beginning with the elusive Jew Dositheus, who was said to have denied the inspiration of the prophets, and ending with Noetus himself. Unfortunately, this work, like so many others of its kind, has perished. All we know of it is told us by Photius, the ninth-century bishop who, luckily for us, took notes on what he read. "Read the little book of Hippolytus; now Hippolytus was a disciple of Irenaeus. The *Syntagma* was against thirty-two heresies, making the Dositheans the beginning, and including those up to Noetus and the Noetians. He says these were subjected to refutations by Irenaeus in lectures. Of these refutations Hippolytus says he made a synopsis and compiled this book" (Photius, Bibl. cod. 121). The meaning of this statement, which Photius undoubtedly derived from the beginning of Hippolytus' work, is (we must agree with Harnack) not clear. But the situation is made even more obscure by the fact that the extant and later work of Hippolytus, the *Philosophoumena*, or *Refutation of All Heresies*, while it actually contains thirty-one or thirty-two heresies, does not begin with the Dositheans and is not by any means a "little book."

On the other hand this *Libellus Against All Heresies*, which was mistakenly handed down among the works of Tertullian, begins with the Dositheans and is an epitome of a work which obviously was not very large. Tertullian did not write it; its style differs markedly from his, and even while he remained in the Catholic church he did not attack the Montanists as this work does. Hippolytus' book is its source; Lipsius proved this in 1865 in his study of the sources of Epiphanius. Philastrius and Epiphanius both make use of the lost work of Hippolytus which this work summarizes. But is this an epitome of the *Syntagma*? It goes only as far as Praxeas, and includes only twenty-five (or twenty-seven) heresies. Nevertheless the last few pages (leaves of a codex?) might easily have been lost. That this is the case seems probable from the awkward first sentence, which was obviously added later in order to connect the work with the *De Praescriptione*, which it follows. Something has been lost in the beginning; therefore, if the work was in codex form, like much early Christian literature, something must have been lost at the end. The beginning included Hippolytus' name and his introduction to the work; the end included Noetus and at least three other heresies after Praxeas, perhaps Gaius and the Alogi among them, as well as the Valentinian Theodotus. There are quite a few who might have been mentioned. The refutation of Noetus, Harnack thought, was to be found largely preserved in Epiphanius.

Pseudo-Tertullian, then, is probably a Latin epitome of Hippolytus' *Syntagma*, his first great work against heresies. As such it deserves our attention; but it is not for that reason that it is translated here. Students of the New Testament and of early Christian literature need a brief and accurate summary of the heresies which vexed the second-century Church. Usually they are presented as so many trends and tendencies or else given in overwhelming detail. Pseudo-Tertullian is brief and to the point. In the notes will be found additional references.

Pseudo-Tertullian Against all Heresies

1. I do not mention the heretics of Judaism, I mean Dositheus the Samaritan, who first ventured to reject the prophets as not having spoken in the Holy Spirit, and the Sadducees, who rising up from the root of his error to this heresy have ventured to deny the resurrection of the flesh. I omit the Pharisees, who are separated from the Jews by their addition of certain items to the Law, from which addition they were made worthy to receive the name which they bear, and with these the Herodians, who say that Herod was the Christ. I turn to those who chose to be heretics from the Gospel. Of these the first of all is Simon Magus, who in the Acts of the Apostles deserved his fitting and just sentence from the apostle Peter. He ventured to say that he was the highest power, that is, the highest god, and that the world was created by his angels, and that he had sought to come down into a wandering demon, which was wisdom, and that he did not suffer among the Jews in the form of God, but seemed to suffer.

This omission of Dositheus is understandable if the *Syntagma* is based on the lectures of Irenaeus, for that writer knows nothing about him. While he probably really lived, for Origen (*Contra Celsum* vi. 11) and Hegesippus (X, frag. 3) mention him, nothing is known of his life. See J. A. Montgomery, *The Samaritans* (1907), 252 *ff*. Simon Magus, on the other hand, was an extremely prominent opponent of early Christianity. The story about him in Acts viii, however, is obviously tendencious, like the tale of Peter's triumph over him in the art of magic in the Acts of Peter. It is strange that our text does not refer to his consort Helena, whom Justin (i. 26) and Irenaeus (i. 23. 2) mention, and whom Hippolytus himself discusses in his later work (*Refutation* vi. 19). The picture of heresy presented in this section is apparently Christian rather than Jewish, for the Sadducees were a party rather than a heresy, and the Pharisees were never "divided from the Jews." The theory of the Herodians given here simply shows to what lengths guesswork in exegesis can be carried. They were, of course, supporters of the Herodian family (A. H. M. Jones, *The Herods of Judaea*, 179).

2. After him his disciple Menander, also a magician, taught the same doctrines as Simon, and whatever Simon had called himself, so Menander styled himself, and he denied that anyone could obtain salvation unless he had been baptized in his name.

According to Irenaeus i. 23. 5, he taught a *gnosis* by which his followers could overcome the world. His baptism, which provided immediate immortality, also prevented old age. Justin (i. 26) tells us that though he taught at Antioch he was born in Galilee.

3. After these there followed Saturninus, and he similarly said that the unbegotten power, that is, God, remains in the highest and infinite regions, the regions above; far distant from this the angels made a lower world, and because a certain effulgence of light had shone down into the lower regions, the angels took charge of creating man in the likeness of that light. Man lay creeping on the earth, but that light and that higher power mercifully saved his soul by a spark. The rest of man perishes. Christ did not exist in a substantial body; he suffered as a phantom. There is certainly no resurrection of the flesh.

Saturninus or Saturnilus taught in Antioch. He was a docetist and ascetic, and held that the God of the Jews was an angel (Irenaeus i. 24. 1 *f*.). Epiphanius develops Irenaeus' hint and says that he and Basilides were pupils of Menander; but this is a common error of ancient historians, who often assume without evidence that to live soon after some teacher is equivalent to being his disciple.

4. Later the heretic Basilides arose. He says the highest God is named Abraxas, the name by which he calls the created mind (in Greek, Nous). Thence came the Word; from it Providence, Power, and Wisdom; from them were made principalities, powers, and angels; thence infinite emissions and emanations of angels; by those angels the 365 heavens were created, as well as the world, in honour of Abraxas, whose name has this number computed in it. Among the last angels, and those who made this world, he places the most recent of all, the god of the Jews, *i.e.* the god of the Law and the prophets, whom he denies to be a god, but calls an angel. The seed of Abraham fell to him by lot, and therefore he brought the sons of Israel out of the land of Egypt into the land of Canaan. He was more turbulent than the other angels, and therefore frequently stirred up seditions and wars, and poured out human blood. But Christ, sent not by this one who made the world but by Abraxas, came as a phantom without the substance of flesh. He did not suffer among the Jews, but in his place Simon was crucified—therefore none ought to believe in him "who was crucified," lest he confess his belief in Simon. He says martyrdoms ought not to be made. He sharply opposes the resurrection of the flesh and denies that salvation was promised to bodies.

Basilides flourished in Egypt in the reign of Hadrian; he wrote twenty-four books of *Exegetics* on the Gospel (see fragments in I above). He claimed to be the disciple of Glaukias, who, like Mark, was an interpreter of Peter, and to have received traditions given to Matthias by the Saviour. His teaching is given much more fully by Hippolytus in the *Refutation* than by Irenaeus; according to Hort (*Dict. Christ. Biog.* i. 268 *ff.*) this fuller version is derived from the *Exegetics* itself, while the version in our Pseudo-Tertullian is that of his followers. The Basilidians used Luke and built a chronological scheme on it. Basilides himself quotes John.

His heresy did not long survive him; probably his followers turned either to Valentianism or to the later orthodox "gnosticism" of Alexandria.

5. Another heretic was Nicolaus. He was one of the seven deacons who were chosen in the Acts of the Apostles. He says darkness was desired by the light, as well as shameful and obscene things; from this mixture came nasty and impure things it is shameful to mention. There are also other obscene matters. He mentions certain aeons, born of evil and embraces and damnable mixtures and mingled obscenities and certain things even wickeder than these. Afterwards demons and gods and seven spirits were born, and other things, sacrilegious and obscene, which we should blush to tell, and therefore omit. It is enough for us that that whole heresy of the Nicolaitans was condemned by the Apocalypse of the Lord, by the very weighty authority of the sentence which says, "Because thou hast this, thou hatest the teaching of the Nicolaitans, which I also hate" [Rev. ii. 6].

It is enough for *us* that the whole heresy of the Nicolaitans was condemned by the Apocalypse of the Lord, for nothing else is known about them.

6. There succeeded to these the heretics who are called Ophites. For they exalt the serpent to such an extent that they even prefer it to Christ. For they say it gave us the origin of the knowledge of good and evil. Noticing its power and majesty, Moses made a brass serpent, and those who looked on it received their health. Christ himself, they also say, in his gospel imitates the holy power of the serpent when he says, "And as Moses lifted up the serpent in the wilderness, even so must the Son of Man be lifted up" [John iii. 14]. They bring it in to bless their eucharist. But the whole occasion and teaching of that error flows from this. They say that from the highest and primal aeon many other lower

aeons have come into existence, but to all these that aeon is superior whose name is Ialdabaoth. He was conceived from the other aeon by mingling with lower aeons, and afterward, when he wanted to go up into the region above, the weight of the matter mixed in him kept him from reaching the higher place, but left in between he spread out completely and thus made the heaven. Ialdabaoth, however, went down lower and made seven sons for himself; he stopped the upper regions from spreading, so that since the angels could not know what was above they might think him the only god. Therefore those powers and lower angels made man, and because he was created by the weaker, mediocre powers, he lay creeping like a worm. But that aeon from whom Ialdabaoth proceeded, moved by envy, sent down a certain spark into man as he lay, by which he might be aroused and grow wise through prudence and be able to understand things above. Thus again Ialdabaoth becoming indignant gave out from himself the power and likeness of the serpent, and this was the power in paradise; in other words, that was the serpent in which Eve believed as if he were the Son of God. She took of the fruit of the tree, they say, and therefore gave the knowledge of good and evil to mankind. Christ was not in the substance of flesh; salvation for the flesh is not to be hoped for.

Irenaeus (i. 30) does not seem to know the name of these heretics, but Hippolytus describes them in *Refutation*, Book V, in great and confusing detail. He includes Naassenes, Peratae, Sethians, and an Ophite writer named Justin. See the chapter in Legge's *Forerunners and Rivals of Early Christianity*, and R. P. Casey, "Naassenes and Ophites," in *Journal of Theological Studies*, 27, 347 *ff*.

7. And then there arose another heresy, which is called that of the Cainites. For they exalt Cain, as if he had been conceived from a certain mighty power which worked in him.

For Abel was created, conceived from a lower power, and therefore was found inferior. These people who assert this even defend Judas the traitor, calling him admirable and great because of the useful services he is boasted to have brought to mankind. Some of them think thanks ought to be given Judas for this reason. For Judas, they say, thinking that Christ was going to overthrow the truth, betrayed him so that the truth might not be overthrown. And others dispute on the other side and say thus: because the powers of this world did not want Christ to suffer, lest salvation be prepared for mankind through his death, [Judas] planning for the salvation of mankind betrayed Christ, so that salvation, which was being obstructed by the powers who stood in the way to keep Christ from suffering, could not be impeded, and therefore by the passion of Christ the salvation of mankind could not be delayed.

Little is known of these heretics; see Irenaeus i. 31, and Epiphanius, *Haer*. 38.

8. But that heresy also came forth which is called that of the Sethians. Of this perversity the doctrine is as follows: two men were created by the angels, Cain and Abel. On this account that power which is above all powers, which they call Mother, when they said Abel was killed, desired this Seth to be conceived and born in Abel's place, so that those angels who had created the two men might become ineffectual, since this seed, the world, arises and is born. For they say that minglings of angels and men were wicked, and therefore that power (which as we said they call Mother) for punishment brought about the flood, so that that seed of mingling might be taken away, and only this seed which was pure might be kept intact. But they who created beings from the earlier seed secretly and surreptitiously, without the knowledge of that Mother virtue, sent the seed of Ham with those

eight souls in the ark, so that the seed of malice might not perish, but be preserved with the rest, and after the flood return to earth and grow, as an example to the others, and spread out and fill and occupy the whole earth. Of Christ they think thus, that they say he was only Seth, and Seth himself was in his place.

Irenaeus includes the Sethians with the Ophites, as does Hippolytus, *Refutation* v. 19 *ff.*; Theodoret, *Haer. Fab.* i. 14, says that the Sethians are called Ophians and Ophites by some people. Salmon and Stählin thought Hippolytus' sources must have been forged documents. Perhaps, as Legge suggests, they were converts' statements from memory.

9. Afterwards Carpocrates introduced this sect: he says there is one power, chief among those above, from which the angels and powers were produced; and they, far removed from the upper powers, created the world in the lower regions. Christ was not born of the virgin Mary, but begotten as a mere man from the seed of Joseph. Of course he was outstanding in his pursuit of virtue and integrity of life. He suffered among the Jews. Only his soul was received into heaven, because it was firmer and stronger than others. From this he deduces that only the salvation of souls is to be maintained; there are no resurrections of the body.

Irenaeus (i. 25) gives a full description of his tenets, and says that his disciple Marcellina, who came to Rome in the time of Anicetus (*c.* 150), made many converts. The Carpocratians worshipped Pythagoras, Plato, Aristotle, and Christ (perhaps also Paul and Homer, as Augustine says), and erected statues of them; like the emperor Severus Alexander, who also included Christ in his house-chapel, they were probably not Christians at all. Their fragments are therefore not given here. They may be found in Clement, *Stromata* iii. 2. 5 *ff.*

10. After him burst forth Cerinthus the heretic, who taught similar doctrines. For he also says the world was created by them; he states that Christ was born of the seed of Joseph, arguing that he was only a man without any divinity, and holding that the Law also was given by the angels. The god of the Jews is not Lord, but an angel.

On Cerinthus see G. Bardy in *Revue Biblique*, 30, 344 *ff*. All that we know of him is to be found in Irenaeus (i. 26, iii. 3, 4). Polycarp told the story that "John the Lord's disciple, going to the bath in Ephesus and seeing Cerinthus within, dashed out of the bath-house without bathing; he said, 'Let's get out! The bath-house may fall down, for Cerinthus, the enemy of the truth, is inside.'" Unfortunately this little story is told also of Ebion and John, of Basilides and John, and of a Christian and a Jew in the second century. We cannot be sure which ones were the original principals. And the reason for the theory of Gaius of Rome that Cerinthus actually composed the Gospel and Apocalypse is completely unknown.

11. His successor was Ebion, who did not agree with Cerinthus in every respect, for he said that the world was made by God, not by the angels. And because it is written, "No disciple is greater than his master, nor a slave than his lord" [Matt. x. 24], he upheld the Law, no doubt in order to exclude the Gospel and vindicate Judaism.

Almost certainly there never was any "heresiarch" named Ebion. The name of this group is derived from the Hebrew word "poor," and the Ebionites were Judaizing Christians of Palestine who retained the Law. Irenaeus (i. 26) says that they used only the gospel of Matthew and did not consider Paul an apostle; he did not keep the Law.

12. The heretic Valentinus brought in many myths; I will condense them and set them forth briefly. He introduces the Pleroma and thirty aeons; he explains them through syzygies,

i.e. certain joinings together. For he says that in the beginning were Depth and Silence; from these came Mind and
Truth, from which burst forth Word and Life, from which
again were created Man and Church. Now from these there
also proceeded twelve aeons, and from Word and Life ten
others. This is the thirtyfold aeon, which is made up in the
Pleroma of the ogdoad, the decad, and the dodecad. The
thirtieth aeon wanted to see Depth, and to see him ventured
to climb into the upper regions; because it was not capable of
the greatness of seeing him it was in revolt and would have
been dissolved unless the one sent to make it firm, named
Limit, had settled it by saying "Iao." That aeon made for
revolt he calls Achamoth, and says that it felt certain passions
of desire and from the passions brought forth matter. For it
was frightened, he says, and afraid and sad; and from these
passions it conceived and brought forth. Hence it made
heaven and earth and sea and everything in them; therefore
everything is weak and fragile and perishable and mortal,
everything made by it, because it was itself conceived and
brought forth from revolt. Yet it created the world from
those materials which Achamoth supplied by dreading or
fearing or mourning or sweating. For from dread, he says,
darkness was made, from fear and ignorance the spirit of
wrongdoing and wickedness, from sadness and tears the wet
materials of springs, rivers, and the sea. Christ was sent by
that forefather Depth, but he was in the substance, not of our
body, but of some sort of spiritual body coming down from
heaven. Like water through a pipe so he passed through the
virgin Mary, receiving nothing from her and not being
changed. He denies the resurrection of this flesh. Of the
Law and the prophets he approves of some things and
disapproves of some; or rather he disapproves of all and
rejects some. He has his own gospel instead of these we
have.

Valentinus flourished about the middle of the second century, when he came to Rome from Alexandria. He was the most influential minority leader we know, with the possible exception of Marcion. He was at once a Pythagorean, a Platonist, and a Christian. On his teaching see E. de Faye, *Gnostiques et gnosticisme*, and F. C. Burkitt, *Church and Gnosis*. The fragments are given in section III above.

13. After him there arose the heretics Ptolemaeus and Secundus, who agree with Valentinus in almost everything and differ only on this point. For while Valentinus fixed the number of aeons at only thirty, they have added several others; they have collected four at the beginning, then another four. And they deny what Valentinus stated, that the thirtieth aeon left the Pleroma as in revolt; for the one which was in revolt because of its desire to see the forefather did not belong to that thirtyfold group.

Of Ptolemaeus we know much more than Pseudo-Tertullian tells us, for Epiphanius and Irenaeus have preserved parts of his biblical criticism. See section V above. Of Secundus we know only what Irenaeus (i. 11. 2) tells us: "Secundus says the first ogdoad is a right-hand tetrad and a left-hand tetrad, and he teaches that the one is called Light and the other Darkness. The power which was in revolt and left the others was not of the number of the thirty aeons, but from their fruits."

14. Then arose another heretic, Heracleon, who agreed with Valentinus, but by a certain novelty of expression wants to seem to have different thoughts. For he holds that in the beginning was that which he calls Lord, then from that monad [proceeded] two, and then the rest of the aeons. Then he brings in all of Valentinus.

Origen's *Commentary on John* is largely a reply to Heracleon's earlier work, and in it we find many fragments of the Valentinian's book (see section VI above). These fragments are marked by the most thoroughgoing allegorization imaginable, though we may admit with E. de Faye (*Gnostiques et gnosticisme*, 101) that Heracleon attenuated his master's system and came closer to the main stream of Christian belief. See W. Förster, *Von Valentinus zu Heracleon*.

15. There did not fail to arise, after these, a certain Marcus and Colorbasus, who composed a new heresy from the Greek alphabet. They deny that truth can be reached without those letters; indeed, they hold that the whole fulness and perfection of truth lies in those letters. For this reason Christ said, "I am Alpha and Omega" [Rev. i. 8, etc.]. When Jesus Christ came down, really a dove descended on Jesus; since its Greek name is peristera it has in it the number 801. They mention *omega*, *psi*, *chi*, *phi*, *upsilon*, *tau*—in fact everything, even *alpha* and *beta*, and figure out ogdoads and decads. To discuss all their vanities would be stupid and tiresome. But what is not so vain, but instead dangerous, is that they imagine another god beside the creator and deny that Christ was in the substance of flesh; they deny the future resurrection of the body.

Marcus' writings seem to have been known to Irenaeus (as Salmon suggests in *Dict. Christ. Biog.* iii. 827), who describes his teaching in considerable detail (i. 13-21). It appears to have much in common with the Jewish Kabbala. His rites included demonstrations of magic: wine became like blood, and with the repetition of the formula, "May the incomprehensible and ineffable grace, which is before everything, fill thy inner man, and make abundant in thee the knowledge of herself, even as she scatters the mustard seed on the good ground," a small cup's contents could fill a larger one. Hippolytus repeats Irenaeus' description and states that he has explained the tricks in Book IV, On Magic; unfortunately his explanation has been lost. Irenaeus also quotes an ode against Marcus by a "divine presbyter and herald of the truth" (see section XV, 3 above). As for

Colorbasus, his existence is doubtful; the name seems to be Hebrew, "the voice of the four," or supreme tetrad, who dictated Marcus' revelations. Irenaeus shows us that the Marcosians, like authors of magical papyri, were fond of Hebrew words.

16. A certain Cerdo is next. He introduces two beginnings, *i.e.* two gods—one good and the other cruel, the good one higher, the cruel one creator of this world. He rejects prophecies and the Law, he renounces the creator god, and he holds that Christ came as the son of the higher god. He denies that he was in the substance of flesh, and says he existed only as a phantom; he did not suffer at all, but seemed to suffer; nor was he born of a virgin—he was not born at all. He approves only of the resurrection of the soul, and denies that of the body. He accepts only the Gospel of Luke, and not all of that. He does not use all the epistles of the apostle Paul, nor does he use them complete. He rejects the Acts of the Apostles and the Apocalypse as false.

According to Irenaeus i. 27. 1, Cerdo was a Simonian; he came to Rome in the time of Hyginus (*c.* 140). To judge from this *Libellus*, which gives the fullest account of it, his teaching did not greatly differ from Marcion's. Possibly, however, some of the latter's views have been credited to his master. Irenaeus also tells us (iii. 4. 3) that sometimes he taught secretly, sometimes he would make public confession in the church, and on at least one occasion he was convicted of false teaching and removed from the assembly of the brethren.

17. After him his disciple arose, Marcion by name, from Pontus, the son of a bishop, who was rejected from the communion of the church because of the seduction of a certain virgin. Since it was said, 'Every good tree bears good fruit, and an evil tree evil ' [Matt. vii. 17], he ventured to assent to the heresy of Cerdo, and to say the same things that the earlier heretic said before.

Marcion's importance may be gauged by the number of works written to refute him. We possess that of Tertullian; but those of Justin, Rhodo, Theophilus of Antioch, Dionysius of Corinth, Philip of Gortyna, Modestus, Irenaeus (?) and Hippolytus are lost. There are also some pseudepigraphical works against him, though probably not so many as is often thought. Marcion distinguished sharply between the God of justice and the God of love, and created a New Testament to support his views. The God of the Jews and the Old Testament he rejected; the Father of Jesus Christ he retained. He was the principal Paulinist of the second century. On his teachings, canon, church, etc., see Harnack's great work, *Marcion* (1924, ed. 2); also J. Knox, *Marcion and the N.T.*

18. There arose after him a certain Lucian, follower and disciple of Marcion; going through the same kinds of blasphemy he taught the same things which Marcion and Cerdo had taught.

Irenaeus tells us nothing of Lucian; to Hippolytus he is only a name.

19. After these there followed Apelles, a disciple of Marcion, who after falling as regards the flesh was removed by Marcion. He introduces one god in the infinite upper regions. He made many powers as well as the angels, and in addition another power, which he says is called Lord but is really an angel. He wants the world to be considered as the creation of this [Lord] in imitation of the world above. He was filled with regret over the world, because he did not make it as perfectly as that world above had been made. He rejects the Law and the prophets. He says that Christ was neither a phantom, as Marcion teaches, nor a being in the substance of a true body, as the Gospel teaches; but because he came down from the regions above, in his descent he wove for himself a flesh of stars and air. In the resurrection, ascending he gave back to the various elements what had

been changed in his descending, and thus when the various parts of his body were dispersed he gave back only his spirit into heaven [*cf.* Luke xxiii. 46]. He denies the resurrection of the flesh. He uses the Apostle, but in Marcion's incomplete collection. He says that salvation is only for souls. In addition he has private and extraordinary texts of his own, which he calls the *Visions* of a certain girl named Philumene, whom he follows as a prophetess. He also has his own books, which he wrote, of *Syllogisms*, in which he tries to prove that everything Moses wrote about God is not true but false.

Apelles, Marcion's best known follower, later founded a sect of his own. He is unknown to Irenaeus, but Eusebius reports a fascinating conversation he had in his old age with Rhodo (section XIX above); Rhodo seems to have won the argument. Several fragments of his *Syllogisms* are preserved in Ambrose, *De Paradiso*, and in Origen (see section XVIII). In these Apelles acutely criticizes the Old Testament narratives. An Apelleiac creed is preserved in Epiph., *Haer.* 44 (XVIII, 11 above). Tertullian, *De Praesc.* 30, says he went to Alexandria after leaving Marcion. In Harnack's opinion this chapter of our *Libellus* used the lost work of Tertullian, *Against the Followers of Apelles*.

20. To these heretics succeeded another, Tatian. He was a disciple of Justin Martyr; after his death he began to think differently. For he understands things entirely in accord with Valentinus, adding [only] this, that Adam cannot be saved: as if when the branches are saved the root is not saved too!

Tatian was a voluminous writer both before and after his lapse into heresy. In the earlier period he composed his still extant *Against the Greeks*, a thoroughgoing attack on Hellenistic civilization, including religion and philosophy, as well as a book of *Problems* in scripture (Rhodo intended to write a book of *Solutions* in reply!) and a treatise *On Animals*. His most important work probably was written later. It was the

Diatessaron, the earliest harmony of the four gospels, of which a Greek fragment has lately been found at Dura on the Euphrates (C. H. Kraeling, *Studies and Documents*, iii). In his thoroughgoing Encratite period he wrote *On Perfection According to the Saviour*.

21. There arose other heretics who are called Cataphrygians, but their doctrine is not single. For there are those who are called Cata [according to] Proclus, and others Cata Aeschines. These have one common blasphemy, and another not in common but peculiar to themselves. The common one is that they say the Holy Spirit was in the apostles but not the Paraclete; the Paraclete said more things in Montanus than Christ set forth in the Gospel—not only more, but better and greater. Those who are Cata Aeschines have this to add: they say Christ himself was Son and Father.

The Cataphrygians, or, as they are usually known, Montanists, were very prominent in Asia after the middle of the second century, especially at Pepuza in Phrygia, where they believed the heavenly Jerusalem would come down. Montanus and his two prophetesses, Prisca and Maximilla, traced their succession back through the daughters of Philip to Agabus, the prophet (Acts xi. 28, xxi. 10); they believed that in Montanus dwelt the Paraclete. Irenaeus does not discuss them as a heresy, for to a certain extent he favoured their views. Later they spread widely, creating what has been called their Diaspora; this Tertullian joined. On them see P. de Labriolle, *La crise montaniste*; W. Schepelern, *Der Montanismus und die phrygischen Kulte*; fragments of an anonymous writer (XXIII) and Apollonius (XXV) above.

22. After all these came Blastus, who tried to introduce Judaism secretly. For he says the Passover must be kept only according to the Law of Moses, on the 14th of the month. Who is ignorant that the Gospel's grace is made void if he reduces Christ to the Law?

According to Eusebius (*H.E.* v. 20. 1) Irenaeus wrote a work *On Schism* against Blastus. He was a Quartodeciman. See G. La Piana, "The Roman Church at the End of the Second Century," in *Harvard Theological Review*, 18, 201 *ff*.

23. There followed these Theodotus the heretic from Byzantium, who after he was arrested for the name of Christ and denied did not stop blaspheming Christ. For he introduced the teaching which called Christ just a man and denied that he was God. While he was born of the Holy Spirit and the virgin, he was only a mere man, superior to others only by the significance of his righteousness.

24. Another heretic Theodotus arose after him; he too introduced another sect and said that Christ was only a man, conceived and born of the Holy Spirit and the virgin. But he was inferior to Melchizedek, because it was said of Christ, *Thou art a priest for ever, after the order of Melchizedek* [Heb. v. 6, etc.]. For that Melchizedek is a heavenly virtue of special grace, because what Christ does for men, becoming their intercessor and advocate, Melchizedek does for the heavenly angels and powers. For he is better than Christ, since he is fatherless, motherless, without genealogy, whose beginning and end is neither comprehended nor comprehensible.

25. But after all these Praxeas also introduced a heresy, which Victorinus [=?] took care to strengthen. He says that God the Father Almighty is Jesus Christ; he argues that *he* was crucified, *he* suffered, *he* died; and with profane and sacrilegious boldness he states that afterwards *he* himself sat down at his own right hand.

These three "Modalistic Monarchians" (23, 24, 25) mark the beginning of the Christological controversies of the third century. See Eusebius, *H.E.* v. 28; Hippolytus, *Refutation*

vii. 35, 36; Epiphanius, *Haer*. 54, 55; and any history of dogma. Tertullian wrote a whole book against Praxeas.

The question may, perhaps, be raised, whether all these names, especially in the period before Irenaeus, really mean anything. A negative answer has often been given, *e.g.* by Köhler (*Die Gnosis*, 5): "Gnosticism has no founders at all; it is a religious mass-movement." But a mass-movement without founders does not produce such a literature as we find exemplified by Basilides' *Exegetics* and the letters of Valentinus and Ptolemaeus. And though we must admit that "Ebion" never lived (his movement was actually old-fashioned Christian Judaism), and that the name Colorbasus is derived from two misunderstood Hebrew words, most of the names which our sources mention stand for real religious leaders of the second century.

SELECT READING LIST

1. *Texts and Translations*

The Ante-Nicene Fathers (9 vol.). New York, 1896-99.

C. Bonner. *The Homily on the Passion by Melito Bishop of Sardis.*
London, 1940.

R. P. Casey, *Excerpta ex Theodoto of Clement of Alexandria.*
London, 1934.

E. J. Goodspeed. *Die ältesten Apologeten.* Göttingen, 1914.

A. von Harnack. *Marcion. Das Evangelium vom fremden Gott.*
Leipzig, 1924.

W. W. Harvey, *Sancti Irenaei episcopi Lugdunensis Libros quinque
adversus haereses* (2 vol.). Cambridge, 1857.

M. R. James. *The Apocryphal New Testament.* Oxford, 1924.

R. Knopf and G. Krüger. *Ausgewählte Märtyrerakten.* Tübingen,
1929.

K. Lake. *The Apostolic Fathers* (2 vol.). Loeb Library, 1913.

H. J. Lawlor and J. E. L. Oulton. *Eusebius* (2 vol.). London,
S.P.C.K., 1928.

H. Leisegang. *Die Gnosis.* Berlin, 1924.

J. B. Lightfoot. *The Apostolic Fathers* (5 vol.). London, 1889-90.

J. C. T. Otto. *Corpus Apologetarum* (9 vol.). Jena, 1842-72.

E. C. E. Owen. *Some Authentic Acts of the Early Martyrs.* Oxford,
1927.

J. A. Robinson. *St. Irenaeus: The Demonstration of the Apostolic
Preaching,* London, S.P.C.K., 1920.

M. J. Routh. *Reliquae Sacrae* (4 vol.). Oxford, 1846-48.

W. Völker. *Quellen zur Geschichte der christlichen Gnosis.* Tübingen, 1932.

A. Lukyn Williams. *Justin Martyr. The Dialogue with Trypho.*
London, S.P.C.K., 1930.

2. *Studies*

W. Bauer. *Rechtgläubigkeit und Ketzerei.* Tübingen, 1934.

F. C. Burkitt. *Church and Gnosis.* Cambridge, 1932.

P. Carrington. *Christian Apologetics of the Second Century.*
London, S.P.C.K., 1921.

C. T. Crutwell. *A Literary History of Early Christianity* (2 vol.).
London, 1893.

M. Dibelius. *A Fresh Approach to the New Testament,* etc. New
York, 1936.

E. de Faye. *Gnostiques et gnosticisme.* Paris, 1925.

E. J. Goodspeed. A *History of Early Christian Literature*. Chicago, 1942.

E. Hatch. *The Influence of Greek Ideas and Usages upon the Christian Church*. London, 1890.

J. Kaye. *Justin Martyr*. London, 1853.

J. Knox. *Marcion and the New Testament*. Chicago, 1942.

P. de Labriolle. *La crise montaniste*. Paris, 1913.

H. Lietzmann, *The Founding of the Church Universal*. London, 1938.

F. R. Montgomery Hitchcock. *Irenaeus of Lugdunum*. Cambridge, 1914.

C. N. Moody. *The Mind of the Early Converts*. London, 1920.

3. *Special Studies*

Chapters XII-XV in the twelfth volume of the Cambridge Ancient History (1939):

F. C. Burkitt, *Pagan Philosophy and the Christian Church*.

F. C. Burkitt, *The Christian Church in the East*.

H. Lietzmann, *The Christian Church in the West*.

A. D. Nock, *The Development of Paganism in the Roman Empire*.

Printed in Great Britain
by
Billing and Sons Ltd., Guildford and Esher
F3556